D0983970

BOYS OF GRIT
WHO NEVER GAVE UP

BY

ELSIE E. EGERMEIER

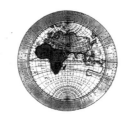

LAMPLIGHTER PUBLISHING
WAVERLY, PA

Boys of Grit Who Never Gave Up.
Copyright © 2003 by Mark Hamby
All rights reserved.
First Printing, September 2003
Second Printing, September 2004
Third Printing, September 2007
Fourth Printing, January 2009

Published by Lamplighter Publishing; a division of Cornerstone
Family Ministries, Inc.

The Lamplighter Rare Collector Series is a collection of Christian
family literature from the 17th, 18th and 19th centuries. Each
edition is printed in an attractive hard-bound collector's format.
For more information, call us at 1-888-246-7735, visit us at
www.lamplighterpublishing.com or write:

Lamplighter Publishing
P.O. Box 777
Waverly, PA 18471

Author: Elsie E. Egermeier

Chief Editor: Mark Hamby
Copy Editors: Darlene Catlett, Deborah Hamby
Layout and Design: Kenn Anderson, Jr.

ISBN: 1-58474-105-8

PREFACE.
by
Elsie E. Egermeier

The stories told in this book are about real, honest-to-goodness boys who became great men. These boys were not different from the boy who will read this. They did not have greater opportunities to make good. But they were wide awake and ready for every opportunity to learn more about the things in which they were particularly interested.

In these stories we see these boys doing the things boys like to do, discovering the things that boys like to know about, and refusing to become discouraged when other persons failed to understand them or appreciate them. Because when they were boys they wanted to do things that are worth something, they became men whom the world calls great.

-THE AUTHOR

What I love most about these true and inspiring stories is the repeated emphasis of a young boy's time that was well spent. Henry Ford was constantly working in his father's barn fixing equipment and learning how things worked. John Wanamaker "kept his mind busy while he worked, always thinking and planning how he might improve himself and get ready to do great things in the future." The Wright brothers, though known for their accomplishments in aerodynamics, also started many businesses together, which required consideration and respect for each other, even as young boys. William Carey would not give up until the entire Bible was printed in six different languages. The lives of these boys who never gave up serve as a reminder that perseverance has rich rewards, especially when one's pursuits are just and for the benefit of others.

Equally inspiring are the accounts of men and women who influenced the character of these boys, as we see in the following testimony:

> *"At seven, my teacher thought I was a dunce and requested that I be removed from the school. But my mother believed that God had a special plan for me. Though I did not have my mother very long, she cast over me an influence which lasted all my life. The good effect of those years that she taught me at home I can never lose. If it had not been for her faith in me at a critical time in my experience, I should very likely never have become an inventor."*
> *Thomas Edison*

Though this is a book filled with inspiring stories of famous boys who never gave up and the powerful influences of those who shaped their lives, it is not entirely about Christian boys. However, the principles brought forth are worthy of following.

Whenever man is the object of emulation, we must be discerning. Whether following Christian or non-Christian mentors, we can learn from their successes as well as their failures. The apostle Paul voiced a similar thought when he said that the Old Testament scriptures were written for our admonition and instruction as well as for our benefit. It is our intention to inspire children to heed the instruction of 2 Peter 1:5-7:

Giving all diligence, add to your faith virtue, and to virtue knowledge, and to knowledge self control, and to self control perseverance, and to perseverance godliness, and to godliness brotherly kindness, and to brotherly kindness love.

It is with great pleasure that I present to you the third volume of *Boys of Grit*. May those stories ignite a fire in the hearts of boys and girls everywhere, to trust God fully and *Never Give Up*!

Mark Hamby
Proverbs 22:4

Contents.

CHAPTER I

"HONEST ABE."

ONE morning a proud little lad clad in his first trousers bade his mother good-by and, pulling his coonskin cap down over his tousled hair, started out to follow the trail which led from his cabin home door into the wide, wide world. He was entering school! A sister, two years older, led the way, and together they trudged along the forest path over a distance of one and one half miles to the backwoods schoolroom. Here they found boys and girls from other cabin homes, and soon the schoolroom hummed to the merry chime of their voices as they memorized the a-b-c's.

Little Abe Lincoln had been born in those Kentucky backwoods on Sunday morning, February 12, 1809. And there he spent the first seven years of his life, playing about the home cabin door, wading in the creek nearby or fishing for "polliwogs" in its sparkling waters, and sometimes following his father into the corn patch to help pull weeds. How grown-up he felt on that first morning when he started to school! And how pleased he was to be able to repeat to his mother in the evening what he had learned in the schoolroom that day! He studied his spelling book faithfully, and before the term ended he was able to spell through it and pronounce the words. Soon he would be reading from a book, like the older pupils. How eagerly he looked forward to that time!

And then something happened which interrupted Abe's school-going for several years. His father decided to leave Kentucky and move into a new territory. So he gathered his few belongings and tied them onto pack horses, then with his wife and two children he rode away over the woodland trail leading to the Ohio River. Doubtless little Abe and Sarah long remembered that weary horseback ride for miles and miles through the woods and over the hills. They had not known before what a big place the world is. By and by they came to the wide River, which they crossed in a ferry boat to the Indiana shore. This, too, was a new experience which they never forgot. Several miles farther they went, before reaching the place where Mr. Lincoln decided to build their new home.

Abe and Sarah were glad indeed to slide off the horses' backs and scramble about through the underbrush, searching for places to build play-houses while their father swung his ax and felled the trees with which he built their new shelter. This shelter was called a "half-faced camp," for it was built of logs against the side of a hill, and there the Lincoln family spent their first winter in Indiana. Mr. Lincoln had to make all the furniture for the shelter from the trees that he cut down, and this took much time. He also had to clear a piece of ground and cultivate it in time to plant his corn. When all of this work was done he began to build a real cabin home, like the one they had left in Kentucky.

Only eight families were living in that part of Indiana when the Lincolns came into the settlement, and their homes were far apart. But soon afterward several other families also came across the river from Kentucky and located in the neighborhood. When their cabins were built, the men set to work to build a school-room to continue their acquaintance with books. Here, as in the Kentucky schoolroom, all the children studied by repeating their lessons aloud after their teacher, and for that reason the school was called a "blab" school. The first book used in this kind of school was a spelling book, and the children were required to spell through the book several times before they began to read. They were also taught how to write and cipher.[1]

A great sorrow came into Abe's life when he was only nine years old, for his mother fell sick and died. There were no doctors or nurses in the settlement, and several other people also died from the same illness. Abe's father was the only carpenter in the settlement; therefore he sawed out the lumber from the trees and built coffins to bury the dead. The sad task fell to him to make such a rough coffin in which to bury his own wife, and as he nailed the boards together his two motherless children stood near him, weeping. No minister was present to help bury her, but several months later a visiting minister came to the settlements and preached a funeral sermon for all those who had died there.

The year after Abe's mother died, Mr. Lincoln went back to Kentucky on a visit, and when he returned to Indiana he brought a new mother for Abe and Sarah; also a stepbrother and two stepsisters. This was the beginning of better days for the Lincoln family, and once

[1] Do mathematical calculations.

more the lonely cabin took on a homelike air, for the new Mrs. Lincoln was kind to the motherless children, and her three children were fine playmates. No one seemed to mind the fact that the cabin was crowded, for they were pioneers and that was one part of pioneer life.

Young Abe grew very fast, and after a while he became a tall, lanky lad, strong enough to help his father clear more land by cutting out the underbrush and chopping down the trees. Then they could cultivate the soil and raise more corn to grind into meal for family use. One autumn he worked for days and days clearing a piece of woodland some distance from the cabin. His little stepsister, Mathilda, begged to accompany him, but her mother refused to allow her to go so far into the deep woods. One morning she slipped away unnoticed and followed along the trail which Abe took. Presently she espied[2] him ahead. So with a desire to take him by surprise, she ran quietly behind. When he stopped, she sprang forward and came in contact with his sharp ax, which cut a gash in her ankle. Abe bound up the wound with bits of cloth which he tore from his shirt and from her clothing, and then, when she had ceased crying, he asked, "'Tilda, what are you going to tell Mother about get-ting hurt?"

---

[2] Caught sight of.

"I'll tell her I did it with the ax," she answered, hanging her head. "That will be the truth, won't it?"

"Yes, 'Tilda, that's the truth, but not the whole truth. Tell the whole truth," he urged; "and trust your good mother for the rest."

Nearly all the people with whom Abe associated in his youthful days were uneducated, and the whole of his schooling was less than a year. But during this time he became a good reader, and books held a strange charm for him. Because the Lincolns were poor they had few books in their possession, so young Abe had to borrow books from his friends to read. Those that he read and reread during his boyhood were, first of all, the Bible, then *Pilgrim's Progress*, *Aesop's Fables*, *Robinson Crusoe*, Weem's *Life of Washington*, and a history of the United States of America. His favorite pastime was reading, and some of his acquaintances who cared little for reading considered him rather lazy because he would spend hours lying in the shade of a tree with a piece of corn bread in one hand and a book in the other. Often he would sprawl on the floor in front of the open fireplace during the long winter evenings and read by the light of the blazing pine knots.

When Abe grew up into manhood, his father decided to move again into a newer country. This time he loaded his family and some of their belongings into a big prairie schooner, hitched two yoke of oxen to it, and turned their faces westward toward Illinois. A slow, tedious journey that was, over frozen ground, thawing roads, and partly-frozen streams. Abe drove the oxen much of the distance. One day when they had forded an ice-coated stream—there were no bridges in that new country—they left their pet dog behind. Not until they had crossed over did they miss him; then they heard him whining on the opposite shore. Looking back, they saw him jumping about in great distress, not wanting to be left behind, yet dreading to plunge into the icy water. The family did not want to forsake him; still they could not afford to waste their time recrossing the stream just to recover a dog. So they decided to move on. But this was too much for Abe. Pulling off his boots and socks, and rolling up his trousers, he waded into the chilly water and triumphantly returned with the shivering little animal tucked under his arm.

After a journey of two weeks, the travelers reached the Sangamon River, about ten miles west of Decatur, Illinois. Here they stopped and began to build a new home. Abe and his stepbrother helped Mr. Lincoln cut down trees to build the cabin; then they helped him clear ten acres of land and plant a field of corn. When this was done, they split rails to make a fence around their field, and during that time Abe was kept too busy to do much reading. Day after day he swung his ax and split the logs into rail lengths; then he helped to build the fence.

Across the river from the new Lincoln home lived a neighbor who wished to build a fence around his premises also. Hearing that Abe was a rail-splitter, he came one day and hired him to help split thousands of rails for him. The wage he offered was small, but Abe was glad to earn a little money, so he took the contract. At another time he split rails to pay for a suit of clothes. He had to split four hundred rails for every yard of homespun cloth used by the woman who made the clothes. And because Abe was a tall young man, his muscles ached before he had split enough rails to make the suit.

But Abe was not content to be a rail-splitter all his lifetime. He felt a desire to become more useful in the world. He loved his country and longed to be of service to his countrymen. When in 1832 the war with the Black Hawk Indians was raging, he enlisted as a soldier and was elected captain of the military company from his neighborhood. But the war was over before his company was called to enter the fight.

River navigation was an important means of transportation during those days, and Abe hired out as a river man on a boat going down the Ohio and Mississippi to New Orleans. He made two trips down the river on flatboats that carried produce to the South. Here he saw for the first time the evils of slavery, and the sight of human beings chained together like beasts, in groups to be sold at the market, touched his heart. He saw them put on the auction-block, where they were sold to the highest bidder. He saw the terror on their faces as they felt the rough hand of their new master, and with a sad heart he turned away. "If ever I have a chance," thought this tall, sober-faced youth, "I shall do my best to end the slave business." And years later it was he who, as President of the United States, issued the Emancipation Proclamation, which set the slaves free.[3]

Abe did not work long as a river man because he believed he could find more important work to do. He spent several years working first at one thing, then another, until finally he became interested in law and politics. Then he decided to become a lawyer. But he knew that lawyers are educated men, and he had no education. This did not discourage him greatly, for

[3] The Emancipation Proclamation set free those slaves who were held in the states which had seceded, not those held in states that had remained in the Union.

he borrowed books of law from a friend and set to work to study them carefully. Then he entered politics and was chosen by the people of southern Illinois to be their representative in the State legislature. This work took him to the State capitol, where he met educated men and women. He learned from associating with them how to cultivate pleasing manners, and he became an interesting guest in the homes of the most cultured people in the city. All the while he continued to learn from studying books and from observing people until he became a prominent man in State politics.

Still Abe was not content to settle down and take life easy. He kept on reading and studying and learning about the needs of his country. He learned about the wrongs that were threatening to destroy the nation, and he longed to help right them. He did not allow the thought that he was only a backwoods boy to hinder him from always trying to do his best wherever he found a place to help.

The time came when the United States of America needed a brave, fearless leader to be their President. And such a man they found in the humble, plodding Abraham Lincoln, for his countrymen believed they could trust this honest man, who was always loyal to the cause of right. On the 4th of March, 1861, he took the oath of office and became President of the

United States. Only a few weeks later his country was plunged into one of the bloodiest wars of its history, for the people of the Northern States and the people of the Southern States fought against each other. This war brought much sorrow to the President, for he loved his country and grieved to see it torn apart. Very carefully he studied the battle-front, and often he sent messages to the generals of his armies. Never once did he give up hope of reuniting the North and the South under the stars and stripes—one flag. So strong was his faith in this united nation that during the war he declared freedom for the slaves who lived in the South. And when the war ended, the slaveholders gave the Negroes their freedom.

Near the close of the war, Abraham Lincoln was re-elected to serve a second term of four years as leader of the nation. But only a few weeks after his second term of office began, he was shot and killed by an enemy. However, he had lived to see the end of the war, for five days before his death the Southern leader had surrendered his arms, and the bloody conflict was over.

And this finishes the brief story of the boy whose life began in a lonely cabin in the back hills of Kentucky and ended in the nation's capital, where he served in the highest office of his country.

CHAPTER II

THE SOLDIER'S SON WHO FOUGHT A STRANGE FOE.

WHAT terror the news of a fresh outbreak of the yellow fever brought to the hearts of the people who used to live in the sunny climes surrounding the Gulf of Mexico and the Caribbean Sea! Hundreds died every year from this plague, and doctors found no successful way to fight against it. Sometimes it broke out suddenly in cities far north of the Gulf, and thousands of people died. Everywhere it was dreaded as a bringer of death.

On the third day of October, 1854, a little boy was born in a fine old Colonial mansion at Toulminville, near Mobile, Alabama, who grew up to fight this strange foe of humanity to the end. His name was William Crawford Gorgas.

Strange as it may seem, if there had not been a yellow fever plague, there might never have been a William Crawford Gorgas! For his soldier father, a young army lieutenant from the North, might never have met and married the charming young woman who became the mother of William Crawford if the terrible disease had not sent them both to the same village in southern Alabama to live as next-door neighbors.

When William was a wee little boy, he used to climb onto his father's lap and examine the shining buttons on his uniform. He used to sit by the hour listening to his father tell of battles he helped to fight in the war with Mexico. And he used to think, "Some day when I grow up to be a man, I too will wear a uniform with shining buttons." A great ambition sprang up in his heart to become a soldier like his wonderful father. Nor did he ever forget it, although he lived to be an elderly man.

Army officers frequently have to move about from place to place, and before William was old enough to start school, his father had served at several army posts. From the sunny South the family had been removed to an arsenal far up in the New England States, where the long, bleak winters seemed cruel to the little lad who loved to play out of doors in the warm sunshine. Later they returned south, locating at the army post in Charleston, South Carolina. Here they were living when the first guns were fired at the beginning of the Civil War. William was then a child of seven years. Sitting with his mother in an open window, they listened to the booming of the guns at Fort Sumter. What a serious time that was! Little William, looking up into his mother's face, said, "Mother, isn't it solemn?"

William's father became a great general in the army to the South during this war. He moved his family to the capital, which was first located at Montgomery, Alabama, and later at Richmond, Virginia. He did not go out to take part in the battles, but he took charge of the department of supplies for the soldiers who went to the front. And a busy man he was! Because William loved his father, he used to spend much time with him at the arsenal, and there he saw all the great generals of the Southern army. Sometimes he helped his father by running errands or by carrying messages.

Four years is a long time to spend in a war-torn country, and William began to see the dark side of warfare. Soldiers moved about in the streets every day who were dressed in ragged clothing and without shoes. Often they were hungry and cold. William pitied them greatly, and he decided to suffer with them. So he refused to wear shoes and ran about barefoot all one winter. In this way he felt that he was becoming a part of the army of heroes whom he admired. Sometimes he went with his mother to carry food to the prisoners, and he helped her carry supplies in her daily visit to the hospitals.

During the war William attended school part of the time, but his schoolbooks did not hold the attraction for him that the military service did. He became a good reader, however, and began to take an especial interest in reading the Bible. Again and again his mother found him lying on the floor with the open Bible before him, perusing its pages. She felt pleased to think that her young son was learning to love God's Word, for she was a good mother. She did not know that William's interest in the Bible was confined strictly to that portion which tells about the wars the Israelites waged against their enemies. Old-time warriors, as well as present-day warriors, were interesting characters to this son of a soldier, who reverenced them one and all.

One busy day General Gorgas paused long enough in his labors to visit the capitol and view the body of Stonewall Jackson, which had been brought from the battlefield. He took

William with him, and together they gazed upon the silent form of the brave man who had given his life for the cause which he believed to be right. William remembered having seen this general at the arsenal, talking with his father. And now he lay cold in death. What a cruel thing war was after all!

The greatest excitement of the entire war period came with its close. The city of Richmond was doomed, for the South was being overpowered. The war could not go on. The army from the North was marching down to seize the city and destroy its capitol. General Gorgas, as a part of the Southern army, was ordered to leave in haste, allowing no time for him to remove his family to a place of safety. Now was William's opportunity to prove his heroism, for his father solemnly informed him that the safety of his mother and sisters rested in his hands. "Should fire break out near the arsenal," his father said, "be sure to remove the family at once to the home of Uncle Thomas. And don't forget to take the cow along." Soon after his father's departure, the city streets became thronged with the incoming troops from the North, and clouds of smoke began to rise above the doomed city. Hurriedly gathering his precious family group together, William started toward his uncle's home, leading the cow by a halter, his mother following with the baby in her arms and four little sisters clinging fearfully to her skirts. They had not gone far when suddenly a terrific explosion occurred, which shook the ground. Every member of that fleeing group remained calm except the cow; she tore at the halter and ran madly down the street, dragging William by the rope. Presently a bit of flying shell hit her and frightened her still more. With a leap she sprang into the air, knocking William down, and when he recovered from the shock, the cow had forever vanished from their sight. Feeling deeply disgraced at his failure to obey his father's parting injunction, William returned to his mother and sisters.

"It's not so bad, Willie," comforted his mother; "just think, that shell might have hit the baby instead of the cow."

But William was not in the proper mood to be comforted. Just at that moment he could not think of anything worse than what had actually happened, so he trudged along with a heavy heart.

Knowing that their home was in ashes, and her husband gone south with the defeated army, Mrs. Gorgas now took her six small children and fled to Baltimore, Maryland to find refuge among her friends. The trip was not an easy one, and years later, referring to it, William said, "I first came to Baltimore a ragged, barefoot little rebel, with empty pockets and an empty stomach."

Some time passed before the family circle could be reunited; then General Gorgas sent for his wife and children to begin their life anew in the sunny Southland. For several years they struggled along, sharing the poverty of their fellow countrymen, for times were hard—especially hard for those who had formerly been accustomed to comfort and luxury. Through these years, William continued his education as best he could, preparing himself to enter college.

Better days came when the General accepted an invitation to become president of the University of the South, located at Sewanee, Tennessee. Here his children had educational privileges which would have been beyond their attainment if they had not lived in the university town, and the following ten years were happy ones for William.

When his college career drew near to an end, the time came for William to decide what he wanted to make of himself as a man. Without a moment's hesitation he expressed his long-felt desire to become a soldier. "Not that, my son," protested his father, who had drunk so deeply of the sorrows of warfare. But William remained firm in his decision; no other line of activity so greatly interested him. Finally his father, seeing how earnestly William longed to carry out his early ambition, consented for him to enter the military training at West Point, where he himself had graduated when a young man. But difficulties now arose which William had not thought of—only on certain conditions can students be admitted at West Point to receive military training, and William could not qualify to meet these conditions!

What looked like certain disappointment now faced the ambitious youth. Still he refused to be entirely defeated, for he decided that if he could not enter the military service as a soldier, he should find some other way to secure entrance. There was the need of army doctors—why not study to become a doctor and qualify for a uniform in this manner? The thought pleased him, so he expressed his desire to his father. At first the General was quite unwilling for William to become an army doctor, but finally he gave his consent, and thus it came about that William enrolled as a student at the Bellevue Hospital College in New York City in the autumn of 1876.

In a short time William discovered, to his own surprise, that he could not have chosen work which he would rather do. No longer was the thought of entering the military service the only motive which led him to his studies; now he studied because he was deeply interested in the work itself. When his father was unable to send money for his needs, he borrowed some from friends and kept right on until he graduated from the college. During those student days, he lived so cheaply that sometimes he actually went hungry, and his clothes showed signs of frequent mending.

After graduating from college, William applied for admission to the Medical Corps of the United States Army. He received his first appointment as army surgeon in 1880, and began his career as army doctor in the southern states. For several years he served at army posts in Texas; then he was sent to Fort Randall, in North Dakota, and finally he was transferred to a remote fort at Pensacola Bay, Florida. During his first years of service in Texas, he encountered the dreaded foe of the South—the yellow fever—and was stricken down with it. But, thankfully for the world, he had a light attack and recovered fully from it. Thereafter he was no longer subject to this strange disease, for persons having it once never suffer a second attack. This enabled him to care for other sufferers without endangering his own life, and often he was sent from one stricken camp to another to minister to yellow fever patients. He bore the distinction of being called a "yellow fever doctor," which meant that, along with ministering to the living, his duty was not infrequently to bury the dead—to even dig the grave, so great was the fear of others lest they became exposed and stricken with the disease.

Then came the Spanish-American War, and William was sent to take charge of a yellow fever camp in Cuba. For many years the capital city of this country, Havana, had been noted as a deadly spot because so many people perished there with this strange disease. Now William cared for the sick soldiers in camp and studied the nature of the sickness, trying to find out its cause. But he got no nearer its secret than did other earnest doctors who studied the disease. They believed the disease to be very contagious, and ordered everything to be burned, even the buildings and the doctors' tools, when the camp finally broke up at the close of the war.

One old doctor who lived in Cuba believed that a certain kind of mosquito was responsible for the yellow fever. He insisted that the sting of this insect would cause sickness, but no one listened to him. William was sent to serve as chief sanitary officer to clean up Havana when the war ended, and he believed the disease germs thrived in filth. Because the city was very untidy, he and his little army of workmen scrubbed it thoroughly from end to end. They dug ditches and installed a good sewer system. When they finally had Havana looking very clean and up-to-date, the yellow fever broke out much worse than it had before. Surely the germs did not breed in filthy places after all.

A company of four doctors now came to Havana, and they began to experiment with the kind of mosquito which the old doctor had talked about. Very carefully they experimented, and they found out that the Cuban doctor was right. The mosquito was the only cause for the strange disease. But what could be done with the mosquito? There were thousands of these insects swarming through the city, especially in and around the buildings. No one knew how to get rid of them. Although the doctors had found out the cause, they did not know how to kill off the pests.

As chief sanitary officer, William now decided to do his utmost to fight this strange foe of mankind. He learned about the habits of this particular mosquito, then he set to work with his army of helpers to make war on them. Instead of guns, he and his workmen carried oil cans, and they poured oil on the surface of all clear standing water, for in such places that kind of mosquito breeds. What a quantity of oil was used in this way! Soon the people found out that William and his helpers were routing the deadly enemy, for yellow fever cases grew fewer and fewer until finally there were none at all. Days, weeks, and months passed, and still no new cases were reported. Then everywhere the news spread that William Crawford Gorgas had made Havana a safe place in which to live.

But Havana was only one of the yellow fever centers in the tropical countries. Other places now needed help, so William was sent to them. First came Panama, that narrow strip of land through which the French had tried to dig a canal to connect the Atlantic and the Pacific Oceans. After nine years' trying, they gave up in despair, for they had dug more graves than anything else. The courageous labors of William and his helpers enabled the United States government to successfully accomplish this great undertaking, for with the yellow fever banished and other tropical sicknesses under control, the Panama country became as healthful as any other part of the world.

Now William had gained the reputation of being a great benefactor of humanity. He had done his greatest work, not in caring for sick folk, but in preventing well folk from getting sick. He had destroyed the cause of one of the most fatal diseases known to mankind. What a noble workman he had been! Because of his accomplishments, he was honored in foreign countries as well as in America. And when on

July 3, 1920, he died on a foreign shore, someone said of him: "They will take him to his own land, but in truth he belongs to us all. He was one of life's greatest helpers, for he cleaned up foul places and made them sweet; and now, as they said of Lincoln, he belongs to the ages."

CHAPTER III

THE SLAVE BOY WHO BECAME
A GREAT LEADER.

HUDDLED together on a pallet of rags that had been spread on the clay floor in a corner of the windowless cabin lay two little black boys, asleep. Presently the younger of them stirred, opened his eyes, and looked about. Something had aroused him. Peering through the dim shadows, he saw the kneeling form of Mammy Jane, her face uplifted in prayer. What was she saying? Little Booker listened, and this is what he heard: "Dear God," prayed Mammy Jane, "here I is, an' my chil'ern, jes' *slaves*. Look on us with pity an' give us freedom, dear God, *please* give us freedom!" So fervently did Mammy Jane pray that little Booker grew wide awake. What could it be that Mammy was wanting so very, very much? He did not understand, for he was only a wee black boy, not yet old enough to know the dreadful meaning of slavery. But from that moment he realized that, whatever it might mean, he and his mother and brother were slaves.

On the large plantation where little Booker lived were many other slaves. Mammy Jane, his mother, cooked for the master and his family, also for some of the slaves who worked in the fields. Long hours she spent every day preparing food for them, and little time had she to minister to the needs of her own growing family. But she loved her children ardently and longed to see the day come when she might walk out from that cabin door a free woman, leading them into a free country.

The plantation on which Booker was born was in Franklin County, Virginia, several miles from a small station called Hale Ford. The date of his birth is not known because no record was kept, but he was only a small child when the terrible war broke out that called so many white men away from their homes to fight. During those years he remained with his mother on the plantation, waiting for the answer to her prayers. And he grew from care-free childhood into boyhood, just like the

other children on the neighborhood planta-
tions, often having little food and less clothes,
for those were dark days of trouble and want
in which both white and black folk suffered.

When Booker grew strong enough, he was
often called from play to run errands, and
finally he grew old enough to take the corn to
the mill to be ground into meal. He would ride
on a horse behind the sack of corn, and thus
carry it to the mill. On the homeward trip he
would have the more difficult task of trying to
balance the sack of cornmeal in front of him,
and sometimes, in spite of his best efforts, the
sack would slip over to one side and fall off.
Then, because he was not strong enough to
replace it alone, he would have to wait until
someone, chancing to pass along that lonely
road, could help him.

One morning in the springtime a messenger
came to Mammy Jane's cabin door and told her
that she and the children were wanted at the
"big house." Every other cabin on the plantation was also visited by the messenger, and
every other slave was summoned to appear at
the same place. So they dropped their work,
like obedient children, and marched in whis-
pering groups to the master's residence. They
knew very well what this summons meant, for
although none of them could read, they had
somehow kept informed about the happenings in the outside world, and for months past

they had known that the great man, Lincoln, had proclaimed their freedom. Still they had pretended not to know, and until the dreadful war closed, they had gone about their daily work as usual. But now that the white men had returned from the battlefields they understood that slavery was at an end and that a new life would begin for them.

Sometime before the war ended, Mammy Jane's husband had gone away to Malden, West Virginia, and there had found work in the salt furnaces. Now he sent a wagon to bring his wife and her children to live with him. This was the first time Booker had left the plantation neighborhood, and the outside world seemed very wonderful to him. But the trip was a long, hard one, for the road led across the rough mountains, and food was scarce. The children walked much of the distance, sleeping at night in the wagon or on the ground. Finally, after several days of travel, they arrived at the little shanty in Malden where they began their new life.

Although Booker could not have been more than eight or nine years old, his stepfather soon obtained work for him and for his older brother in the salt furnaces. One day he saw a young man reading a newspaper to a group of listeners, and he, too, edged his way into the circle to listen. How wonderful it would be, he reasoned, if he could read. But Mammy Jane could not teach him, for she had never handled a book in her life. Neither could her husband, for he did not know how to read. Regardless of this, Booker made up his mind that somehow or other he *must* learn, and he told his mother of his great desire.

About this time a gentleman who came into the neighborhood opened a school for colored children. Mammy Jane got a book for her son, hoping to start him off with the other children, but her husband felt that Booker could not be spared from his work. So a disappointed little lad, hiding his tears as best he could, trudged on to the salt furnaces, while the other neighbor children learned their a-b-c's in school. "Never mind, honey," comforted his mother, "you'll learn some day." And Booker decided that his mother was right.

Day after day the little black boy had seen barrels of salt packed in the mines and marked with certain letters. By watching these closely and by asking questions, he learned the letters, and before very long he could read as well as some of the children who went to school. Then, after a while, his stepfather consented to let him go to school half a day if he would get up early in the morning and work as much as possible before school time. This he did willingly, rising so early that he could be off to work at four o'clock in order to quit in time to be at school by nine o'clock.

Although Booker's first day in school was the happiest day of his life, it brought a strange embarrassment to him. He noticed that when the teacher called the roll, every child had two names. He had only one. Therefore he decided to choose a surname for himself. So when the teacher asked for his full name, he replied, "Booker Washington."

One Sunday morning, as Booker and some other boys were playing marbles in the road, an old colored man passed by on his way to Sunday school. He stopped and talked to the boys, telling them that they ought to go to Sunday school too. Until this time Booker had never heard of a Sunday school, but he grew so interested in the old man's description of the school that he put his marbles into his pocket and started to Sunday school that very morning. Thereafter he attended regularly, and when he grew older he taught one of the classes. Finally, when he became a young man, he superintended the Sunday school.

Booker's first school days did not last long, for the poverty-stricken condition of the family made it necessary for him to spend whole days at work. About this time his stepfather sent him to work in the coal mines. What a horror came into his heart when, for the first time, he entered the dark, damp shaft that led far back into the mountain! But he took his book along, and in spare moments he tried to read by the light of the little lamp which hung on his cap. Not long afterwards his mother hired someone to teach him at night, hoping thus to encourage her boy. But the new teacher was poorly educated and unable to teach him very much.

Mammy Jane, however, was not discouraged. She kept looking about, and finally she found a place where her son could work as a houseboy. His new employer was a woman, and at first Booker thought she was very strict. He had never been taught the necessity of neatness, cleanliness, and order, for his own mother, having had no opportunity to learn these things, could not teach them to her children. But she urged him to learn all that he could from this good woman, and after a few discouraging experiences Booker began to appreciate his new employer. While in her employ he continued to take time to study, sometimes attending school in the afternoons, and the rest of the time engaging a teacher at night.

After spending four years as houseboy, Booker decided to go to the Hampton Institute, in Virginia, and continue his education. He had heard that in this school poor students were given an opportunity to work for their board, and with such an opportunity he felt sure that he could secure an education. But the journey to Hampton presented many difficulties; he had not enough money to pay his railroad fare all of the way, so had to walk a part of the distance.

The first task assigned to Booker at the Hampton Institute was that of sweeping a classroom. How thankful he was then for the careful training he had received under his strict employer when he worked as houseboy! Now he knew how to sweep and dust as well as a trained janitor, so he did his very best. And the principal of the Institute was so well pleased with his work that she said, "I guess we will try you as a student." He continued to do his best at work or with his books, and in three years' time he graduated with the regular class.

Because his older brother had helped to pay his expenses, Booker decided that now he should earn money to help pay his brother's way through the Hampton Institute. So he returned to his home town and began to teach school. For three years he continued there as a teacher, in both day and night school, besides conducting two Sunday schools on Sunday. Then he spent another year in study at the Wayland Seminary, in Washington, D.C., still struggling to prepare himself better for a place of usefulness in the world. Just what that place should be he had not yet decided, but he knew that in order to be his best in any place he should secure as good an education as possible. For a time he thought of becoming a lawyer, so he began to study law in earnest. But after a while he felt sure that he could do more good in the world as an educator of his people; so he gave up his study of law.

From this time Booker thought a great deal about the problem of helping his people. Less than twenty years had passed since he, a little ignorant ex-slave lad, had marched with them into the land of freedom, and now, unknowingly, he was fitting himself to become their leader. He saw that millions were still ignorant and poor, needing someone to teach them how to help themselves become useful citizens of the great country they loved so dearly. And he decided to do his very best to help as many as he could. Then one day a call came from the South for an educated man to organize a Normal school[4] for colored students, and Booker Washington answered that call.

At Tuskegee, Alabama, Booker found a group of earnest people, white and colored, who wished to establish a school at that place in which to train educational leaders for

---

[4] A two-year school for training elementary teachers.

the colored race. He listened to their plans and encouraged them to go ahead. So they appointed him as principal of the Normal school and opened summer school in an old church-building and a little shanty that was almost ready to fall down from decay. These buildings they gladly furnished as best they could with necessary school equipment, and on July 4, 1881, Booker Washington began in earnest his great life work as an educator of his people.

From this humble beginning the Tuskegee Normal and Industrial Institute grew, under the leadership of Booker T. Washington, into the greatest training center for colored students in the South. Here the yearly enrollment, numbering thirty students during that first summer term, grew into thousands of young men and women who came from all parts of the South to better fit themselves as teachers and trained workmen. These great results did not accomplish themselves, but came about through the untiring labors of the founder of the Institute and his faithful helpers.

Booker Washington's remarkable ability as an educator and his unselfish devotion to his life work drew the attention of millions of people and won for him many lasting friendships among the best citizens in the world. He was welcomed into the social circles of the kings and queens of Europe during his vacation abroad, and everywhere he was treated with the greatest respect. Accomplished as an orator, he was invited to address audiences numbering thousands of people in various parts of America, and always in simple, forceful words he spoke of the longing of his heart to help his fellowmen become honest, respectable, worthwhile citizens of the great Republic.

After spending thirty-four years in ceaseless work for the uplifting of his race, Booker Washington's tired body wore out, and he was laid to rest beneath the sunny skies of the Southland that he loved so well. But the great work which he began and urged forward is still going on as a living monument to this truly noble man.

CHAPTER IV

The Boy Whose Dreams Came True.

THE Revolutionary War had just ended, and the brave commander of the American army, General George Washington, was the hero of the hour when, in the home of Deacon Irving, on William Street, New York City, a baby boy was born. "The child shall be named after Washington," said his mother, who hoped, as all fond mothers do, that her son would grow up to honor his country.

When six years later General Washington returned to New York City to become the first President of the United States of America, little Washington Irving wished very much to see the great man whose name he bore. One day while he was down town with his Scotch nursemaid, Lizzie, the President passed by and entered a shop. "Now is my chance," thought Lizzie, knowing how much her youthful charge wished to meet the President, so she led him quickly into the shop, and, approaching the dignified gentleman, she said, "Please, Your Honor, here's a bairn[5] was named after you."

President Washington looked down kindly into the shining eyes of the little lad who stood before him; then he placed his hand upon the child's head and gave him his blessing. Long afterwards, when little Washington had grown to manhood and had become famous as America's first author of international reputation, he remembered the glad thrill he felt when the President spoke to him that day. And among the best books that he wrote was a story of the life of the first President of his country.

The New York City in which the Irving family lived when Washington was born, April 3, 1783, was hardly bigger than a town. Its dusty streets, lined with Dutch and English houses that faced wooden sidewalks, led away from the water-front. Here and there at convenient street-crossings were town pumps where the people came to get their daily supply of water

---

[5] In Scotland and northern England, a young child.

for home use. The main street was not much more than a mile in length, and the side streets had the irregularity of country lanes. Still, this was one of the most important cities in the whole of the United States, and as such it was chosen to be the seat of the government, the capital city of the new nation.

Little Washington was the youngest child in the family, and sometimes his parents and his brothers and sisters and even the nurse were too busy to watch him closely. He would slip through the door, run down the dusty street, and disappear out of sight. On and on he would go until he came to the end of the street at the water-front. Then he would follow the road that led to the wooden piers and scramble onto these bridge-like structures, which were built far out into the water. Sometimes he would sit down on the edge of a pier and swing his little bare legs above the deep water. Sometimes he would lie down flat on the rough boards and look up at the sky, then out toward the big ocean where the ships came sailing in. He would watch the sail-boats and the flat-boats and the frigates enter the port, and he would wonder where they came from. He would watch the sailors unload their vessels and reload them again with different produce to carry away to some other land. And then he would think and think about the time when he would be a grown-up man, big enough to sail away from home in a ship to a faraway country. Sometimes he would forget to go home, and then his parents and brothers and sisters and the nurse would have to search everywhere to find him. Even the neighbors would help them take up the search, and the town-crier would go up and down the streets calling out, "The deacon's son is lost! Has anybody seen the deacon's son?"

We do not know what happened to little Washington when "the deacon's son" was found, for the deacon was a very stern father. Maybe he sent the little run-away sobbing off to bed without any supper—maybe.

By and by, when Washington grew old enough, he started to school with his brothers and sisters. And there he learned how to read. Soon he was able to read such stories as *Robinson Crusoe* and *Sinbad the Sailor*, and these stories made him think more about the great wide world which stretched so far away to other lands across the sea. He felt that he could hardly wait until he would grow up and become a sailor, for then he could travel all over the world, seeing things. When he was told that sailors are poor men, that they have to work hard and live without home comforts and eat rough foods, he still wanted to become a sailor. "I shall train myself when I am a boy," he thought; so he began to sleep on the bare floor at night instead of in his warm, soft bed. And he tried to eat salt pork, the kind that the sailors must eat. But because he was not a healthy lad, he soon had to quit his training, for eating salt pork made him sick and sleeping on the bare floor caused him to catch cold.

Although Washington liked to read books of poetry and travel, he did not like to study other books. He did not care to go to college as his older brothers had done but wanted to stay at home and study only the kinds of books which interested him. This was not wise, and after he grew up he felt sorry that he had refused to attend college. He had to work much harder because he was not well prepared to do his work. He began when only a schoolboy to write verses and short stories for his own amusement, but he did not plan to become a writer of books.

When Washington grew older he liked to shoulder a musket and go out into the woods and fields with his brothers or chums to hunt wild game. One summer he spent his vacation in a country place called Sleepy Hollow, not far from the Hudson River. Because he was a friendly lad, he became acquainted with the farmers who lived in the Hollow and went hunting in their fields and woods. What a wonderful time he had! Years afterwards he wrote an interesting story about that place which he called "The Legend of Sleepy Hollow." And because the story was published and read with great interest, the lonely country place which it described became a famous spot.

One by one the Irving brothers and sisters grew up and married and moved away to other homes. Washington was sometimes invited to visit them. These visits took him to new places, and everywhere he went he looked about to find interesting people and sights. One time he went to visit his married sister who lived in the Mohawk Valley, up the Hudson River. He had to travel in a sail-boat that slowly made its way around the bends of the river between the green hills and along the foot of the Catskill Mountains.

What interesting sights he beheld as he lay on the deck and watched the ever-changing shore line! Sometimes screaming eagles would soar overhead; sometimes the boat would glide under the shadow of stern cliffs rising up from the water's edge; then around the bend they would pass where new scenes lined the river-banks. At night the boat would anchor near the shore and wait until dawn to continue the journey upstream through the highland region to the Mohawk Valley beyond. So greatly did young Washington enjoy the scenery along the way that years later he described some of it in his famous story called "Rip Van Winkle."

Washington was now fast growing into manhood, so he had to begin making plans for the future. He remembered his early longing to become a sailor, but he was not strong enough to endure such a rough life. So he decided to study law and prepare to become a lawyer. For several years he spent a part of his time in a law office, reading books and thinking that some day he would be a lawyer. But often he would have to leave the office and spend long hours in the out-of-doors, for he needed to breathe the pure, fresh air of the country and to exercise his muscles to gain strength. In these out-of-door excursions he would some-times follow the Hudson River and wander off toward the Catskill Mountains, enjoying the beauties of nature along the way. Perhaps he feared that he might be wasting his time dur-ing these long, pleasant tramps away from the office. He did not know that they were better preparing him for the life he would live by and by—that he would never be a lawyer after all.

Everywhere he went he kept his eyes and ears open to see and hear interesting things, and these things he remembered. When the time came for him to write, he described in pleasing language the sights and sounds of these wanderings. And people in far-away countries, reading his stories, seemed to see the things he wrote about and to hear the sounds he described. Thus they came to appreciate the scenery along the beautiful Hudson River and in the mysterious Catskill Mountains, and America became to them a country of interest.

Instead of growing stronger Washington grew weaker every year, and finally his brothers decided that he needed to take a trip across the ocean to recover his health. They knew that he was interested in seeing things, and they hoped that the climate of other countries might restore his health. So they furnished the money that he needed and sent him away to Europe. When he stepped into the sailing-vessel that was to carry him across the ocean, the captain saw him. "There's a young chap," thought he, "who will die before we get to Europe. We will have to bury him in the sea."

But the captain was mistaken, for instead of growing weaker Washington began to regain strength, and at the end of the six weeks' voyage he was much improved in health. He did not have to travel like a sailor, working hard and eating rough food. As a passenger on the ship he could sleep in a fairly comfortable cabin and eat the best kinds of food. He could spend the long daylight hours sitting idly on deck or walking about in the open air visiting with his fellow passengers. He realized now that his childhood dream to become a world-traveler was beginning to come true, even though he could not be a sailor. And how happy he was!

At Bordeaux, France, the sailing-vessel came into port, and young Irving stepped into a strange country. Even the language which the people spoke was not very familiar to him, for when a lad in school he had not cared to study other languages. Now he wished that he had been a better student. He had to work very hard before he could speak French well enough to go about and enjoy visiting the interesting places in that country. He also learned how to read the language so he could study the literature of France. Then with some companions he started across the country toward the Mediterranean Sea, stopping in villages as well as in cities to see the sights and to get acquainted with the people.

Italy was the next country he visited, and here he won more friends, for everywhere he went he made himself agreeable and made the best of his surroundings. "When I cannot get a dinner to suit my taste I endeavor to get a taste to suit my dinner," he wrote good-naturedly to his friends back home.

One day while in Italy, he boarded a Genoese packet[6] and sailed away to the island of Sicily, in the Mediterranean Sea. On the way the packet was attacked by a pirate vessel

_____
[6] A small ship that carries mail, passengers, and goods regularly on a fixed route.

and robbed. What an exciting experience this was to the young traveler! But no harm came to him. When they reached the island he set out to explore the ruins of some ancient cities. Sometimes he traveled through dangerous stretches of country where robber bands often attacked travelers. But he passed through safely. One time he came to a part of the country where he found half-starved people living in wretched cabins or in caves along the hillsides. He had never seen such poverty and misery before, and the memory of it troubled him long afterwards.

On his homeward voyage, Washington stopped for a while in England, where he won more friends among a people who spoke his own language. This country seemed familiar to him because he had heard so much about it ever since he could remember. He enjoyed sightseeing in England among the historic places that he had read about in his schoolbooks.

By this time Washington's health was quite restored and his purse nearly empty, so he bade his friends in England good-by and sailed back across the Atlantic to America. His brothers were glad to see him looking so well again, and now they expected him to settle down and go to work. They thought he would become a lawyer, but the law office held no attraction for him. Finally, when assisting his brother in some literary work, he began to write a humorous story which he called "Knickerbocker's History of New York." This story he published in a book, and everywhere it was read with interest and delight. Even in England, among the most highly educated people, the book was well received and the youthful author was on the road to fame.

Several years later Washington had a chance to help his brothers who had been so kind to him. These men failed in their business and needed money to make a new start. Washington decided to write another book and thus earn some money with which to help them. So he wrote *The Sketch Book*, which is the most famous of his works. The great success of this book surprised him, but he did not grow proud of himself. Instead he worked all the harder to use his talent well.

As Washington grew older he studied more diligently and planned to write books of historical interest. He wished to write about the life of Columbus, the discoverer of America, so he sailed to Spain and studied Spanish literature. Then he wrote several interesting stories about the early history of Spain, as well as a book about the life of Columbus. The style of his writing pleased the people so well that they honored him as a great author. His writings still rank among the best literature.

Finally, Washington Irving returned to America, after having spent many years in other countries as a traveler and a student. He was welcomed home by his countrymen, who were proud of the honors he had won. Soon he settled down in his home at Sunnyside, on the banks of the Hudson, to spend the last years of his life among his kinsfolk and friends. There he wrote several more books, the last of all being his *Life of Washington*.

At the ripe old age of seventy-five years, Washington Irving laid down his pen and took one more journey, this time into the land that lies beyond the river of death, from whence no traveler ever returns.

CHAPTER V

The Boy Who Wanted His Country to Produce a Famous Poet.

ONE day an old man sat alone in a library, working away busily with pen and paper. But every now and then his thoughts were disturbed by shouts of childish laughter, which came floating up to him through the open window. Finally he pushed his work aside and turned to gaze out of the window and watch the children at their play. Then, with a smile on his lips, he returned again to his table, selected a clean sheet of paper, and scribbled on it some hurried lines. Here are a few of them:

> *Come to me, O ye children!*
> *For I hear you at your play,*
> *And the questions that perplexed me*
> *Have vanished quite away.*

Come to me, O ye children!
And whisper in my ear
What the birds and the winds are singing
In your sunny atmosphere.

For what are all our contrivings
And the wisdom of our books
When compared with your caresses
And the gladness of your looks?

This old man was Henry Wadsworth Longfellow, whom we call "everybody's poet," because everybody who reads his poems enjoys them. They are so greatly appreciated that some of them have been rewritten in foreign languages, to give the people in other lands a chance to read them and enjoy them, too. Thus the people in sunny Italy, and in Spain, in snow-clad Scandinavia, in far-away China and India, and in nine other foreign countries are able to read Longfellow's beautiful poems in their own languages.

Because Mr. Longfellow was one of America's greatest poets, and the first to receive pleasing attention from people in foreign countries, we are interested to learn about his boyhood and early life before he became famous.

In the city of Portland, Maine, on the 27th day of February, 1807, Henry Wadsworth Longfellow was born. At the time of his birth the United States was only beginning to

make a place for itself among the nations of
the earth, for the stars and stripes had been
flying only a few years "o'er the land of the
free, and the home of the brave." But already
the United States was finding out that it must
prove its courage and purpose to the peoples
of other lands, for it had waged war against
the pirate state of Tripoli, and had convinced
those half-savage people that the United States
of America is a nation not to be trifled with.

During the war against Tripoli, a brother of
Mrs. Longfellow's served as a naval officer in
the army, and near the close of the war he was
killed in the explosion of a fire-ship before the
walls of Tripoli. When Mrs. Longfellow first
looked upon her newborn son, she thought
about her brave soldier-brother who had been
killed, and she decided to call her baby by his
name. So Lieutenant Henry Wadsworth's name
lived again, this time in the form of a little boy
who was destined to grow up and become a
peace-loving man and a famous poet.

When Henry was only three years old, his
mother sent him to school with his slightly
older brother, Stephen, and there the two
small boys learned the alphabet and how to
put the letters together to spell words. From
their babyhood the sight of books was familiar
to them, for their father was a lawyer and a
student. Often they had seen him spend the

long winter evenings around the home fireside with his books, and they grew up to believe that books are worthwhile possessions. Their mother, too, was fond of reading, and she encouraged the children to study. No wonder, then, that Henry began to think about writing words to print for others to read when he was still a boy.

When Henry was only five years old, another war waged in which his country took an active part. During this war, his home town, which was situated on the seacoast, needed protection from the enemy's ships. So Uncle Sam sent some ships up to the Portland harbor. While they were there, a sea-fight took place off the coast. How excited everybody must have been! And how anxiously they must have watched and listened to find out how the fight was coming on! Finally the enemy's warship was captured and brought into the harbor by the United States *Enterprise*. Long afterward, Henry wrote a poem in which he mentioned this event in the following manner:

I remember the sea-fight far away,
How it thundered o'er the tide!
And the dead captains, as they lay
In their graves, o'erlooking the tranquil bay
Where they in battle died.
And the sound of that mournful song
Goes through me with a thrill;

> *'A boy's will is the wind's will,*
> *And the thoughts of youth are long, long*
> *thoughts.'*

At the age of six Henry entered the Portland Academy, already knowing how to read, write, spell, add and multiply numbers. That he was a bright, studious little fellow we may well believe from what his teacher, Mr. Carter, wrote of him at that time: "Master Henry Longfellow is one of the best boys we have in school. His conduct last quarter was very correct and amiable."

But Henry did not spend all his time in the schoolroom. Sometimes he went with his mother to visit in the country, and the great out-of-doors he greeted with boyish delight. He liked to roam through the fields, to jump fences, to wade in the brooks, to climb trees, and, as he grew older, to explore the deep woodlands. He loved to listen to the song of the birds, to the chirp of the crickets, to the sight of the wind in the tree-tops, and to the sound of the waterfalls. He loved to watch the sunrise and the sunset, and sometimes he would lie down on the soft green grass and watch the fleecy clouds sail by in the blue heavens. How dreamily they floated along, assuming odd shapes which now and then resembled people, or animals, or fantastic objects. And sometimes, too, he would join his mother by a window during a thunderstorm to watch the play of lightning streaks across the angry sky.

One day, when Henry was thirteen years old, he wrote a poem which he believed was good enough to print in the city newspaper. So he sent a copy of it to the editor of the paper, and then watched anxiously to see if it would appear in the poet's corner. Sure enough, after some time he found the poem just as he had written it, occupying a part of the column in the poet's corner. How happy he felt! But when his father failed to notice it or at least to make any remarks about it, young Henry felt somewhat disappointed. Nor had the worst happened yet. That same evening he went with his father to visit Judge Mellen, who lived near by, and whose young son was Henry's playmate. While there, the judge picked up the newspaper and commented on the poem. What he said about it did not sound the least bit flattering; in fact, he criticized it very freely. Poor Henry! He heard every word, and not one bit of self-defense could he offer. Nor did his father attempt to cheer him. So he returned home, minus the pride which he had carried about in his heart all the day. And a tearful, wounded little lad he was when he fell asleep.

But Henry did not allow the first bitter discouragement to drown his ambition to write poetry. There seemed to be something within him urging him to make rhymes out of his thoughts; sometimes they seemed to sing themselves into rhythmic measures with scarcely any effort on his part. The spirit of the poet-to-be was waking up! He became more interested in studying poetry; he read with greatest interest the wonderful poems which had been written by such men as Shakespeare, Tennyson, and Scott. He knew these writers were natives of Great Britain, and he longed for the time to come when America would produce a poet of true worth. He believed that his native land had just as much music in her brooks and rivers as could be heard in the waters of Great Britain, and he felt certain that a true poet could find as interesting things to write about in America as could be found in any other country in the world.

One day Henry found in an American magazine a poem written by an American citizen named William Cullen Bryant. This poem pleased him very much, for it seemed to breathe the spirit of his native country. From that time he watched for Bryant's poems, and he enjoyed reading about the birds and flowers and prairies and forests of his own beloved America.

But Henry was not yet ready to turn all his attention to poetry. He needed to continue his studies a while longer. With his brother Stephen, he took the entrance examinations from Bowdoin College when he was only fourteen years old and made passing grades. A year later the two brothers enrolled as students of the college in Brunswick, Maine, and set to work in earnest. Here Henry found opportunity to prepare himself better to become a writer, and occasionally he sent a poem to the leading magazines to be published. No longer were his writings criticized by his elders, for those who read his poems were pleased with them.

One of Henry's fellow students in college was a young man named Nathaniel Hawthorne. Nathaniel and Henry were both greatly interested in reading good books. They also liked to walk about in the beautiful woods near Brunswick and observe the curious habits of the wild little creatures who made their homes in the trees and bushes. Henry read about the Indians, who used to be at home in the Maine woods, and he carefully studied their customs. Then, when Exhibition Day arrived, he represented in a debate an American Indian talking with an emigrant from England. Nathaniel also studied nature as well as his books, and later he also became famous as a writer.

Henry believed that his father wished to have him study to become a lawyer after he should finish his education at Bowdoin College. But he did not want to become a lawyer, so he wrote to his father, telling about his desire to become a writer instead. And he was greatly pleased when his father consented for him to follow his own choice of a life-work. This meant that he would have to study for several more years; also that he would have to leave his beloved country and travel for a time in other lands, studying the customs and languages of other people. But he did not mind the hardships of study and travel; he wanted to prepare himself well to do the work he had set out to do. He knew that he could not expect to become a great writer unless he worked hard and spent long hours over his tasks. So he bravely set out to climb the long, long road that leads to success. And this is what he wrote about that climb:

> *We have not wings, we cannot soar;*
> *But we have feet to scale and climb*
> *By slow degrees, by more and more,*
> *The cloudy summits of our time.*
> *The heights by great men reached and kept*
> *Were not attained by sudden flight,*
> *But they, while their companions slept,*
> *Were toiling upwards through the night.*

When Henry returned from his travels in Europe, he became Professor of Modern

Languages in the same college where he had graduated a few years before. He taught French, Spanish, and Italian, and had to prepare his own textbooks. This work kept him very busy, and for a while he seemed to be forgetting the great desire of his heart to become a poet. But he could not forget completely, because the longing to write returned again and again until finally he had to plan his work so that he could devote some time to writing. Often he would sit up late at night to write a poem; sometimes he would waken from sleep with his mind full of new thoughts that rhymed, and then he would rise early and arrange those beautiful thoughts on paper.

When Henry was still a young man, the University of Harvard, in Cambridge, Massachusetts, appointed him Professor of Modern Languages. So he left the little village of Brunswick in his home state and came to Cambridge to teach. Here he lived for many years, until his children grew up and married and their children came to play about in the warm sunshine beneath his window.

One day as Henry was walking down Brattle Street in Cambridge, he saw a blacksmith standing in front of his shop beneath a chestnut tree. He noticed how strong this man looked, how hard he worked, and how much good he accomplished as day after day he kept blowing his bellows and swinging his heavy sledge upon the anvil. He stopped to chat with the blacksmith and to ask questions about his work. Then when he returned home, he wrote a poem about "The Village Blacksmith." This poem was published in newspapers and magazines until nearly everybody in America read it. Finally it was reprinted in schoolbooks, and the American children saw the beautiful word-picture of the spreading chestnut tree and the blacksmith shop beneath it.

Then one day the leading men of Cambridge decided to widen Brattle Street, and in order to do this they would have to cut down the chestnut tree. The poet of Cambridge, however, did not want that tree cut down; he tried to persuade the city mayor and his friends to spare the tree. Although they appreciated the great old man who loved the tree, they would not let it stand. But they planned a nice surprise for Mr. Longfellow. They invited the children of the public schools to build out of the wood of that tree, by their small subscriptions, a beautiful armchair for him. This unexpected gift pleased Mr. Longfellow very much, and he sat in it one day and wrote a poem of thanks to the children. He placed the chair in his study and invited all the boys and girls to come and see it. And what a gay procession of youthful visitors that invitation brought!

Mr. Longfellow's interest in the American Indians caused him to write "The Song of Hiawatha," a beautiful poem which has been rewritten in many languages. The Indians, too, were pleased with this poem, and years after the poet died they invited his daughters to their reservation to see them perform scenes from "Hiawatha" in the forest on the shores of the "big sea water" of Lake Huron.

At the age of seventy-five years, Henry Wadsworth Longfellow died, but the beautiful poems which he wrote continue to live on and to keep their established places among the best literary classics. And so it happened that he who, when a boy, wanted his country to produce a famous poet, grew up to become that famous man himself!

CHAPTER VI

The Boy Who Became An "Empire Builder."

IN what unlikely corners of the earth kind Providence finds material out of which to build great men! Here and there, from cities, plains, and wildernesses He makes His choice, often finding in homes of the lowly a child whom He sets apart for some noble service. And then, with unerring hand, He guides that willing one across trackless plains, over all kinds of seeming obstacles, through discouragements, on and on to the goal ahead, where his great life work must be done.

Material for the making of such a willing worker Providence found in a little log house at the edge of the Canadian wilderness, forty

miles from Toronto, Canada, when James
Jerome Hill was born, on September 16, 1838.
Though living far from the city, surrounded
with the influences of pioneer life, James's father
decided that his young son should receive an
education and fit himself for a place of usefulness in the world. So he sent little James at an
early age to the district school, where the child
learned that books are made not just to show
pictures, but to teach knowledge. And there
his education began.

In spite of the long, cold winters and the
deep snows of that northern clime, little James
continued his studies at the district school
until he was eleven years old. Then his father
placed him in a private school called the
Rockford Academy, where he spent four more
happy years with his schoolbooks. Here the
teacher was a highly educated Quaker gentleman who encouraged his pupils to seek for the
best things in life by fitting their minds for all
that might come to them in future time. "Train
yourself to think, to plan, and to make use of
opportunities to do bigger things," he used to
tell the boys and girls whom he taught. And
because James greatly admired the professor,
he believed it would be worthwhile to try to
follow his instructions.

At the age of fourteen James's schooling
came to an end, for he became an orphan and

had to do his own thinking and planning for the future. He remembered the advice of his beloved teacher to think, plan, and make use of present opportunities to prepare to do better and bigger things, so he resolved to put this into practice. Now that he had to make his own living, he looked about to find something to do. Not far from his home was a country store where a bright boy was needed to help about the place. Here James found work not long after his father died, and for nearly four years he clerked in the store.

During these years, James thought a great deal about what he should do when he grew up to manhood. He did not want to keep a country store all his lifetime; neither did he want to be a farmer. The great, wide world seemed to beckon him to seek his fortune afar. Finally he decided to become a sailor, so bidding his friends and the storekeeper good-by, he started for the United States. He had only a little money, the savings of his salary for clerking at the country store, but he knew how to get along with very little because he was trained in pioneer life.

First he went to the Atlantic coast and visited several seaport towns, wishing to enlist as a sailor. But nowhere did he find things just as he fancied they would be. So he changed his plans and turned westward, intent on going to the Pacific Ocean. What a long, dangerous journey that would be! No railroads crossed the continent at that time, and beyond St. Paul, Minnesota, travelers had to push their way across vast stretches of uninhabited plains where warlike Indians still prowled about in ravines, ready to pounce upon the white men without a moment's warning. James hoped to reach St. Paul in time to join a band of troopers and traders who were starting for the West. But when he arrived at the little trading settlement, as St. Paul then was, he found that he had come too late.

As soon as he learned that no more bands would start westward before the following spring, owing to the lateness of the season and the impossibility of overland travel through the winter months, he decided to remain there and wait. While looking about for something to do, he noticed that the life of the settlement was centered around the Mississippi levee, where the steamboats came and went, bringing shipments from the South and carrying Northern produce down the river. Soon he found employment as a clerk on the levee for J. W. Bass and Company, agents for the Dubuque and St. Paul Packet Company of the Mississippi River steamboats.

James worked for his new employer only a short time when he found that the shipping business was full of interest. He learned everything that he could about it, and studied the maps to see where shipping products came from and where they were sent. He also studied engineering, history, and science in his spare moments. He was finding out that although he could not continue his education in college, he might still become an educated man if only he would make use of good books and magazines. He tried to remember the things he read about and to use the knowledge he gained in this way.

In the little frontier settlement this orphan boy was surrounded by many temptations to carelessness and wrong-doing, and he might have easily drifted along in company with evil-minded persons. But he remembered the teachings of his early days, and the fact that his father wished him to fill a place of usefulness in the world encouraged him to do right. Although his father was dead, James resolved to try his best to grow up into a strong, clean man—the kind that his dear old father might have been proud of. So after the day's work was over, he would spend his evenings in the good company of books, or else he would engage in the interesting pastime of making water-colored drawings.

By the time the winter's snow had disappeared and the frozen ground had thawed out and dried, more westbound travelers arrived in St. Paul. But when they set their faces toward the wilderness, following the overland trail, James was not among their number. During the long, cold winter he had thought seriously about his plans to go farther west and had decided that it would be better to remain in St. Paul for a while. Later on, when he would be able to plan bigger things, he would go. Until then he would continue his work and his studies and become better acquainted with the needs of that undeveloped country lying between St. Paul and the Pacific Coast.

In the wheat-growing sections of the country surrounding St. Paul, the farmers depended on the old-fashioned cradle scythe to cut their grain, for the threshing-machine had not yet been introduced among them. One day a salesman came to town and asked James's employer to take the agency for the threshing-machines. "We will ship the machines to you," explained the salesman, "but you will have to set them up for the farmers."

Turning about, the employer asked, "Hill, do you think you could do it?"

"I might," replied James, "if first I could see one at work."

And sure enough, after watching a threshing-machine operate in a wheat field not far from town, James came back and put the parts of a new machine together just where they belonged. In a few days a farmer came to town and bought the machine, putting it to work at once, and it worked successfully.

From reading the newspapers, James learned that there was talk of building a railroad across the United States, from coast to coast. He became much interested in this undertaking, for he believed the wilderness country would be opened to settlement more quickly if some better means of transportation were provided for its settlers. While working as clerk for the shipping company, he used to think about the possibilities of a shipping route west and north from St. Paul. A bigger business could be carried on and the country would develop faster. One day, while helping load a steamboat, he remarked to a fellow worker, "We are loading steamers now, but it will not be long before railroads will take their place."

"I guess you're dreaming, Jim," laughed his companion. "You'll not live to see those new-fangled railroads crowding out the steamers. No sir!"

"Wait and see," replied James, quietly.

Several years passed by, and James kept steadily on at work. But all the time he continued to think and to plan about the big things that needed to be done for the Northwest. One day he came to his employer and said, "At the end of this month I am going to quit here." His employer had been pleased to see how thoughtfully James applied himself to the work, and he felt unwilling to lose such a reliable young man.

"I will increase your salary if you will stay with us longer," he said.

"No, thanks," replied James; "you are paying me enough for my work. I am quitting here because I want to start a shipping company of my own."

"Don't do that," urged his employer. "There are too many shipping companies here for you to make a success of another one. You will not be able to make even a living at it."

But James was not discouraged with this kind of advice. He had studied the shipping business carefully, and he believed that he understood it well enough to make a start. So in company with a partner, he went into business on his own account.

Now he began to think more seriously about opening up new shipping routes and doing a bigger business. One day he said to his partner, "What would you think of opening up a line north to Winnipeg, across the Canadian border?"

"The idea!" exclaimed his surprised friend; "you might as well think of opening a direct line through to Japan."

"I hope to do that some time," answered James, leaving his partner to guess whether he meant it or not. But James did mean just what he said. Not long afterward he established, by means of a regular line of boats, carts, and steamers, a shipping line which operated between St. Paul and Winnipeg, called the Red River Transportation Company.

Owing to his careful planning and work, James found time to enlarge his business interests still further. He studied the conditions of the country and urged the building of more railroads through the State. Finally, he found an opportunity to help do this work himself, for he and four of his friends bought the St. Paul and Pacific Railroad Company. At that time the company had only two lines built and a few started. Besides that, there was an indebtedness of thirty-three million dollars. But six years later there was a finished track laid through to the Red River, connecting with the government line to Winnipeg. Then the shipping industry could be carried on north by means of the railroad instead of by boat and cart, as in former times.

The great Northwest still seemed to call to James, who remembered his early ambition to go to the Pacific Ocean. Now he planned to build a railroad in that direction. So, taking with him a French-Indian guide, he left St. Paul and started west to learn the exact conditions of that part of the country. He knew an abundant supply of coal would be needed to operate the railroads, so he looked about and found where coal could be obtained. He then planned how he might control these coal mines when the time would come that he would need them to carry on his work. And years later, when the need arose, he was ready to go ahead with other plans.

James made several trips into the wilderness to learn what he could about that big, open country. Sometimes he and his guide traveled on foot, wearing snowshoes; sometimes they rode in a sleigh. Occasionally they would take a boat and travel a long distance up the Missouri River. On these journeys across the country, James would think about the great changes which would take place when a railroad would connect these out-of-the-way places with the rest of the world. He would gaze far out across the wind-swept plains and think how different they would look when the homesteaders' houses would be dotted here and there, surrounded by fields of waving grain. For he believed that men and women eager to build homes in a new country would flock westward as soon as it became possible for them to make a living on homesteads and have a way provided to ship their farm products to other parts of the country.

The time came when James saw these very things happen. For he built a railroad called the

Great Northern through Minnesota, Dakota, and across the unsettled plains of Montana, then across the mountainous region to the sea. Many years passed by before the last rail of that track was laid, and James Hill was now a man of whom his country could feel proud. For in spite of discouragements he had kept on until he had made his youthful dream come true.

Even with all this accomplished, James Hill was not ready to quit. He remembered that as a boy he had dreamed of going to see the Oriental countries. Now he decided to send ships to those countries, carrying produce that would benefit the people. First he sent some men to study the needs of those people, and when he learned that they wanted flour and steel from America, he built two huge ships, called the *Minnesota* and the *Dakota*, and sent them across the Pacific with loads of produce. At last he had opened a direct line of transportation through to Japan, just as he had told his surprised partner many years earlier that he hoped to do some day.

James Jerome Hill earned his title, "Empire Builder," first by planning and building a road over which people might travel quickly and safely to begin life in the wilderness, then, by encouraging them to use better methods of farming, he helped them to become satisfied in their new homes. By and by other people came, and still others, until towns and cities sprang up along the Great Northern Railroad, and thus the empire of the Northwest became a reality instead of only a dream.

CHAPTER VII

THE ADVENURES OF ANDY, THE LITTLE HIGHLANDER.

SCATTERED throughout the cities of America are grand monuments in the form of public libraries that celebrate the memory of one fine old man who only in recent years has been called away by death—Andrew Carnegie.

Three miles inland from the sea, on the eastern coast of Scotland, stands the once famous old town of Dunfermline, where kings and queens used to reside in the long ago, and where the ruins of their old castle still remain. This town also holds the honor of having been the birthplace of "our Andy." In the attic of a one-story house on Moody Street of this town, little Andy first beheld the light of day on November 25, 1835. The only child at home and the first baby in a circle of warm-hearted uncles and aunties meant that Andrew received a great deal of flattering attention from them. And so he grew from babyhood into childhood beloved by them all. He won his way into the hearts of the neighbors and friends of the family by his sunny smiles and happy disposition.

When still a very little boy, Andy moved from the small house where he had been born to a larger house in a better neighborhood. His father's business was growing, and the change became necessary. Andrew's earliest memories took him back to this second home, which was reached by an outside flight of stairs leading from the pavement. And his earliest recollection was that of seeing a map of America on rollers in his new home, his parents and two other relatives earnestly gazing upon it. Soon afterwards those relatives sailed away to America to build a home for themselves in a strange land.

For a while Andrew's father continued to do well in his business as a linen weaver, but the time came when steam machinery was introduced to take the place of the hand looms which Mr. Carnegie used. This meant that Mr. Carnegie, with his four or five hand looms, could not produce as much at as cheap a cost as the weaver who used steam machinery. And from that time Andrew's father began to fail as a businessman. Because another member had entered the family circle—a baby brother named Thomas—Mr. Carnegie's family expenses were increasing while his business profits were falling off. Like the brave woman that she was, Andrew's mother found some way to help earn money and to teach her son that honest work is honorable. Soon little Andy was doing his bit to help along by carrying water from the town pump and running errands from the shop.

The people of Dunfermline believed that every child should receive at least a start on the road to learning, so by the time Andy was six years old his little playmates were going to school. He did not go, nor did he seem to care. His parents, however, cared a great deal. They wished to send him to school along with the other children, but because they had promised never to send him until he would ask to go, they waited with great uneasiness for him to ask. Finally, to help matters along, they told their troubles to the schoolmaster, who was a kindhearted man, and asked him please to take an interest in little Andy. Not long afterwards the master invited Andy to go with him and a class of boys on a hike into the country. Of course Andy went, and, as his parents hoped, he came back so pleased with the master, Mr. Martin, that he asked to be permitted to go to school.

And what an interesting place the school-room proved to be to this little light-haired Scotch laddie! Here he soon took his place beside the children of his own age, although he had enrolled a year later than they. His lessons became a delight, and his grief lay in the fact that sometimes, because he had to carry water from the town pump, he was too late at school to attend the first class. It was not that he did not get up in time to carry the water before school opened—not that. But the supply was low, and the water was not turned on until so late that Andrew could not fill his pail and carry it home in time to reach school by nine o'clock. Mr. Martin understood why he was so often tardy, and he did not chide him. Some of the other pupils, seeing this, began to call Andy the "teacher's pet." And those unkind words made a sore spot in his heart.

Although Mr. Martin was the only school-room teacher that Andy ever had, there was another who, in his childhood, helped him a great deal to become studious. This other one was his Uncle Lauder, whose only child Andy called his cousin-brother "Dod." These two boys were often together, and Dod's father used to entertain them by the hour telling them stories. He chose to tell stories about the history of Scotland and to picture the heroic deeds of Scotland's brave men in the minds of his youthful listeners. As a result, both Andy and Dod grew familiar with the history of their native land, and they became ardent hero-worshipers of those men who had dared to die for Scotland.

Just outside the town of Dunfermline was a wonderful park enclosure which in earlier days belonged to the palace grounds of the kings and queens. This place was closed to the public, and only occasionally through the gates did Andy catch a glimpse of the beautiful scenery that lay inside the high walls. His thought of heaven was linked with that enchanting ground, so near and yet forbidden. Also there stood in his home town an ancient tower called the Abbey, built by King Robert the Bruce[7] as a last resting-place for the rulers of Scotland. From the top of this tower the curfew bell rang each night at eight o'clock, and its pleasing chimes furnished music for the town citizens. How many little Scottish lads and lassies were tucked into bed each night to the music of the curfew bell! Andy loved to listen to the ringing of the chimes.

But times continued to grow harder for

---

[7] Robert I, King of Scots (1274-1329).

the Carnegie family, and finally the parents decided to sell their home, their hand looms, and all their furniture, bid good-by to their beloved Scotland, and sail away to the "land of opportunity," as America seemed to be. This was a sad day to twelve-year-old Andy, for he believed no place on earth could be quite so dear as the highlands of Scotland. Through tear-dimmed eyes he watched the scenes familiar to his childhood fade from view as they rode away. Then as they went on board the ship that was to carry them across the wide Atlantic, Andy threw his arms around his Uncle Lauder's neck, and bursting into tears he cried, "I cannot leave you!" But soon afterwards, when the ship sailed away, Andy was on board with the rest of the family, for he knew his father and mother were determined to begin life in America, and that he must go with them.

Life on board that sailing vessel proved to be a grand experience to Andy. He quickly made friends with the sailors, and the seven weeks' voyage passed by happily for him. He was permitted to help with their lighter tasks and, as a reward, was invited to share their Sunday dinner dessert—a rare treat this was, indeed. No wonder that Andy was sorry when the shores of America loomed in sight, warning him that his ocean ride was near its end!

For a short time the Carnegie family remained in New York, visiting friends in that city. Then they started farther west, to Pittsburgh, Pennsylvania. Once more they traveled in a boat, going by way of the Erie Canal, through Lake Erie, down another canal to the Ohio River, and upstream to Pittsburgh. Three weary weeks they spent on this inland waterway trip, which requires less than ten hours' by rail nowadays.

At the end of the tiresome trip, their hearts were gladdened when once more they were reunited with the relatives who had left Scotland for America when Andrew was a tiny boy. Now these kind relatives, knowing of the poverty of the Carnegie family, furnished them two rooms free of rent in which to begin their new life in America. So they located in Allegheny City, near Pittsburgh, and there little Andy, the Scottish highlander, grew up to be a full-fledged American citizen.

Attending school was quite out of the question for Andy, as his parents were too poor to buy books. Little Thomas was not yet old enough to enter the primary grades. So the first weeks passed by drearily in the strange new land. Finally Mr. Carnegie found work for Andrew as a bobbin-boy in the cotton factory where he also worked. On winter mornings they rose long before daylight, ate their breakfast, and were off to work before the sun was up. All day they toiled in the factory, with only a little time off for the noon-day lunch, returning home after dark each night. And at the end of the week, Andrew received for his toil only one dollar and twenty cents. That was a hard life. But Andy loved his parents and longed to help them secure a home of their very own. He knew that every penny he earned would help a little in caring for the family expense, and this kept up his courage. He hated poverty and resolved to find some way to climb out of it as quickly as possible.

Not long after Andy started to work there, a Scotchman who manufactured bobbins needed a boy in his factory and offered to pay Andrew two dollars a week if he would run a small steam-engine and fire the boiler in the cellar of his factory. This work was even more disagreeable than the work Andrew was already doing, but it meant more pay—and that would help the family more. So Andy took the job and started in, bravely determined to make the best of it. When tempted to be discouraged, he would think about the brave heroes of Scotland who endured all kinds of hardness for the sake of the cause they believed to be right, and this would help him to keep bravely on in the ill-lighted, sooty cellar. One day his employer needed someone to help make out some bills. Finding that Andy could write well, and also that he understood arithmetic, the man asked him to do the work. Thereafter Andy was relieved from the work of running the steam-engine, to keep books for his employer. At once he decided that he should know more about his new work, so he and three of his friends enrolled in a night school to study the larger system of bookkeeping.

One evening when Andy came home from work, he heard that a messenger boy was wanted in the telegraph office over in Pittsburgh, nearly two miles away. His uncle, who was a friend of the manager in the telegraph office, had recommended Andy for the place. At first Andy's parents feared that he was too young to become a messenger-boy, for the wages—two dollars and fifty cents each week—they believed were intended for an older person. Andy then was only fourteen years old and was small for his age. However, he pleaded with them to let him try, and finally they consented.

Dressed in his Sunday clothes, Andy walked with his father over to Pittsburgh early one morning to apply for the work. Then leaving his father in the street, he climbed the stairs to the manager's office and made known his errand. Mr. Brooks, the manager, thought that Andy looked a bright, willing lad, so he agreed to hire him.

"When can you begin work?" he asked.

"Right away," was Andy's quick reply. And right away the manager gave him some work to do. But we may be sure that the first message he delivered was to his father, waiting in the street below. At his first opportunity he rushed down the stairs and shouted merrily, "It's all right! Go home and tell mother I have been hired."

The telegraph office, with newspapers, pens, and pencils lying about, and with sunshine streaming in at the windows, seemed like heaven compared with the gloomy cellar where Andy had worked in the bobbin factory. He set to work in earnest to learn all that could be learned about his new work. He helped do the janitor work in the office, sweeping the floors and dusting the furniture. He delivered messages wherever he was sent, and in spare moments he watched the telegraph operator send and receive messages over the wire until he learned how that work was done. Finally, he too became a telegraph operator.

During this time, a well-to-do citizen of Allegheny—Colonel Anderson—opened up his private library on Saturday afternoons to working men and boys who wished to read and improve their education. Andy was very glad for this opportunity to borrow and read good books. Soon he was learning about the history of the United States of America, and about our heroes who had lived and died for a country as dear to them as Scotland had been to him. He was studying the best kind of literature, reading biographies of great men, and finding out what an interesting place the great wide world is, in which he shared a part. He never forgot the kindness of Colonel Anderson in sharing his library with the public, and years later he followed the example of this kind man by opening public libraries in many cities for the benefit of people everywhere.

While still a boy, Andy helped his parents pay off their debts and buy a home for themselves. He was always careful not to spend his money foolishly and to keep his eyes open to opportunities for earning more. By the time he grew into young manhood, he had worked so faithfully and studied so hard that he became superintendent of a railroad. He continued to work and to plan, as an honest man, until he became very, very rich.

Then Andy looked about for opportunities to use his money wisely and make other people happy. He visited his boyhood home in Scotland, and one day he bought the beautiful palace grounds near his home town and turned it into a public park where boys and girls might romp and play. He bought the old tower with the curfew bell, too, and he built in the town the first public library building. In America he gave millions of dollars to build schools, hospitals, and libraries. And always he remained a true friend to the working men, for he remembered the days when he had toiled so hard as a working lad. He learned to love America, "the land of the free, and the home of the brave," but often he would return to visit the highlands of Scotland. He traveled in many other lands also, getting acquainted with many notable people. And everywhere he manifested sympathy for the poor and a deep interest in the happiness of his fellow-men.

CHAPTER VIII

The French Boy Who Thought Things Through.

EVERY bottle of pasteurized milk left at our doorsteps is a silent reminder of the great man, Louis Pasteur, who gave his life to make the world a healthier, happier place in which to dwell.

The birthplace of this great man was a humble dwelling in the quiet village of Dole, France, not far from the Swiss border. His parents were called peasant folk in France. They were plain, humble people. His father had once served in the army of France under the great Napoleon and was a loyal patriot. But when he laid aside his sword to build a home, he engaged in the tanning trade to make a living. He married the daughter of a market-gardener who lived near the tannery, and Louis was their first child.

"The greatest things in quiet places grow," wrote one poet when referring to the growth of the great oaks from the tiny acorns, "and men are like the trees." So little Louis, who grew up to become a great scientist, began his life in a quiet village home. Like all fond parents, the Pasteurs believed their child was a wonderful lad, and they wanted to give him a chance to grow up into a wonderful man. They believed he needed a good education, and although they were poor, they began to plan for this before he was old enough to enter school.

Not far from Dole was another town, Arbois, where a tannery was located near the Cuisance River. In this town was a splendid school, just the kind suited to the needs of a beginner such as was Louis. So his parents moved to Arbois in order that he might enjoy the privileges of this good school. Already they had taught him the alphabet, for his father could hardly wait until Louis might learn how to read. Using the French a-b-c's, they had taught him how to spell words for them to pronounce when he was just a wee boy.

In the primary room of the Arbois college, Louis enrolled as a beginner and found himself one of a group of scholars who spelled words aloud in a sort of sing-song. Their teacher divided them into groups and appointed one in each group to instruct the younger members. Although Louis was the youngest member in his group, he wished very much to become the one chosen to teach the others. So he studied his lessons very diligently until he was able to recite without making a mistake. At home he found his father always eager to help him with his lessons. One thing Louis especially liked to do when a small schoolboy was to buy new lesson-books and proudly write his name on the first page. Every new book meant that he was advancing further in his studies.

When Louis was not at school, he liked to play about in the tannery yard. What great fun he and his chums found in dodging about among the pits that had been dug in the yard for the preparation of skins for tanning! Sometimes he and his friends would go down to the river near by and catch fish. But Louis seldom went far from home to play. The tannery yard, he believed, was the best playground of all, and there he could hear whenever his parents called him to run an errand for them.

Louis was a thoughtful little fellow in the schoolroom. He always wanted to be very sure that he understood his lessons before passing on to new ones. Because of this unwillingness to rush ahead, the teachers considered him slow, but his father was pleased. "Louis will understand every page he turns," said his father proudly. Every evening in the Pasteur home found Louis and his father bending over the lesson pages and reviewing the lesson for that day. In this way Mr. Pasteur had an opportunity to study also. As a little boy he had been denied such an opportunity to go to school, and now he was glad to be a student with his little son. Just as long as Louis attended school near home they shared every lesson together, and when he first went away to college, he sent copies of each lesson home. When the time came that Louis had advanced so far beyond what his father could understand without a teacher's explanations, the proud old father continued to feel deeply interested in everything that Louis was studying.

At the age of fifteen Louis was ready to enter a school of higher learning than the college of Arbois. One of his instructors, the headmaster of Arbois College, had been urging him to study to become a professor. Often they had walked about the college grounds together, and Louis had listened with sparkling eyes while the headmaster told of the bright future which might await him if only he would continue his studies in Paris.

But Louis' father was too poor to send him to school in Paris. Besides, he felt unwilling to part with his son. He wondered how he could live without having Louis near by. Then he remembered that some day Louis would be a man, ready to do a man's work, and he knew it would be unwise for him to refuse to let the boy continue his education and prepare for a useful life. "Louis must fill a more important place in the world than I am filling," reasoned his father; "and I must help him get ready for that place." So when friends offered to make arrangements to lessen the expense of his schooling in Paris, Mr. Pasteur consented for him to go.

Never afterwards could Louis forget that bleak October morning when he bade his parents and little sisters good-by and set out on the tedious journey to Paris. He had to travel in a crowded stagecoach to the Nation's capital with only one school companion to accompany him. Neither of the boys had been so far from home before, and both of them felt lonely and unhappy. Unlike many other boys, the love of adventure did not lure them away from the scenes of childhood, and the gravest kind of homesick feelings began to tug at their heartstrings when they watched the familiar landscape fade from view and strange country scenes open before them. Finally, after the last change of horses, the coach came galloping into Paris.

"Here," thought Louis, "I shall study so hard

that I will be able to forget my longings to be at home with my father and other loved ones." But try as he might, he could not overcome his homesickness. He could not eat, he could not sleep except to dream of the folks at home, and he could not study as he had studied when attending the college at Arbois. Everything was strange and new, and he could not accustom himself to the change. "If only I could get a whiff of the tannery yard," he told his friend one day, "I feel that I should be cured." But there was no tannery yard near by. When several weeks passed his instructor grew uneasy lest Louis should become really ill, so he sent word to the boy's parents.

Not many days later someone called to Louis and said, "They are waiting for you close by." Not knowing whom to expect, he went to the waiting-place indicated, and there found a man sitting at a small table, his bowed head in his hands. Just one look at the stooped form of the man and Louis recognized his father. With a glad cry he sprang forward, for he understood that his father had come for him.

Sure enough, Mr. Pasteur had been just as unhappy because of the separation as Louis had been. So the two journeyed back to the village home, and Louis decided to study to become an artist instead of a professor. Already he had shown an unusual talent for drawing, and this seemed to be the kind of work for which he was best suited. He enrolled once more at the Arbois College and set to work in earnest with his paints. In a short time he advanced so far that his instructor could teach him no more. And he could not become even a successful artist without receiving more education!

Once more the kind headmaster of the college talked to Louis about his future work. "Art is good," said he, "but I feel that you could do better than become an artist. Try again to continue your other studies, for surely you can succeed."

Not long afterwards Louis enrolled in a college not far from his home town, where his father frequently went to buy and sell skins. He knew the visits of his father would help keep up his courage; and besides, he was now growing old enough to realize that some day he would have to look the world in the face all alone. So he bravely set out, determined to conquer.

In the new school Louis took a keen interest in his studies. He liked to experiment with chemicals, and one day he performed his first scientific experiment by extracting phosphorus from bones. Later on, when he became a professor, he encouraged his pupils to prove by experiment in the schoolroom what they had learned from the textbooks.

Before Louis could become a professor, he needed to take some training in Paris. So he returned the second time to that city and entered school. No longer did he suffer from homesickness for he had decided to prepare himself to teach science, and he knew that he must study hard and long in order to do that. Often he wrote long letters to his parents and sisters telling about his life in Paris and about the experiments he was making in the classroom.

One day after Louis had been experimenting for a long time, he made a discovery which drew the attention of noted scientists from other countries. News of this success came to the Pasteur home and brought joy to his loved ones. But he did not become proud of his success. He kept right on, trying to find other discoveries which had never been known before.

Many people then believed that such creatures as lizards, flies, bees, etc., mysteriously grow out of thin air. Louis knew they must be mistaken, for no living thing can come from the emptiness of nothing. So he proved by his experiments that such a belief is only superstition. However, he did discover that the air contains millions of tiny living organisms called germs, which cannot be seen with the unaided eye. He proved that these germs, too small to be seen without a microscope, often cause the worst diseases among people and among animals. He experimented very carefully to prove these facts. Then he found the way to prevent much of the suffering and death from cruel diseases that were formerly spread by germs.

The people of France began to realize that Louis Pasteur was a great man indeed. When disease threatened to destroy their cattle or sheep, they sent for him to come and find out what caused the disease and what would prevent it from spreading among their flocks and herds. Always he went, for he was a friend of his countrymen, willing to serve wherever he was needed most.

One day a call came from the southern part of France. This time he was wanted to save the people in a stricken district from poverty. They depended on the silkworm industry for a living, and their silkworms were dying by the hundreds. Some strange disease, which they could not understand, was threatening to ruin their business. Louis had never studied worms and knew nothing of their habits. But he answered the call from those distressed people and went to see if he could help them. First he had to study the silkworm; then he learned what was causing the disease that killed so many of them. For many months he experimented before he was able to learn the right thing to do. But in the end, even the king and the queen of France honored him because he had kept the country from financial ruin.

As Louis Pasteur grew older he thought more about helping suffering people. He discovered the secret of pasteurization, which has become a blessing to the world in that it prevents much sickness and death.

But the distressing disease whose mysterious cause haunted him was hydrophobia. No one had ever found a successful way to treat this terrible disease. Every person or animal affected with it suffered the worst agony, and there seemed to be no cure. Louis decided to find a cure, so he first studied the disease by experimenting with rabbits and dogs which had hydrophobia. Very carefully he had to handle them lest he get bitten himself. After making many tests, he discovered a way to prevent animals that were bitten from getting sick and dying. Then he wanted to see if the experiment would work with people as well as with animals. Fearing that this might be a dangerous experiment, he thought he would not endanger the life of anyone else but experiment on himself. He intended to allow himself to be bitten and then to subject himself to the same method of cure which he had successfully tried with bitten animals. But before he had time to do this, a call suddenly came to him to treat a nine-year-old boy who had been severely torn by a mad dog on his way to school. The boy's parents had heard about the success of Louis' experiments with bitten animals, and they believed that he could save the life of their child. So they rushed him to Paris, and Louis undertook his case. Several weeks' time was required in order to complete the cure, and during this time Louis cared for the boy very tenderly. At the end of the time of treatment the boy was cured and was able to return home well.

This was a great triumph for Louis. Afterwards he was called to treat other persons who had been bitten by rabid wolves or by other mad animals. Some people came even from other countries to receive his treatment and be cured.

Louis Pasteur lived to be seventy-two years old, and until the end of his useful life he kept busy studying how to help other people. He received the highest marks of honor from the rulers of France and tokens of esteem from other countries. But always he remained the same quiet, earnest, energetic man, ready to help wherever he was needed.

CHAPTER IX

The Boy Who Translated The Bible Into Many Languages.

"Though his beginnings be but poor and low, Thank God! A man can grow!"

IN a hollow at the end of the village of Paulers Pury, Northamptonshire, England, stood a plain little cottage where lived a poor weaver and his young wife. One late summer day in 1761, their humble home was gladdened by the birth of a son whom they named William.

For six years little William Carey's smiles and childish prattle brought sunshine into the plain little cottage in the hollow while his father toiled at the hand loom weaving cloth or worked in the garden near by. Then one day, the mover's wagon came and carried everything away from the place to unload it before the door of the schoolhouse that stood on the hill up in the village. Little William understood that his father, Mr. Edmund Carey, was to become the future schoolmaster of the village and that he would be permitted to attend school. At that time there was no public school free to all the children of the village; only a few were granted the privilege of a free education. And because William's father was one of the educated men of the village, knowing how to read, write, and cipher, he was chosen to take the place of the teacher who had moved from the village to another town.

The schoolhouse was, in reality, a dwelling house in which the master and his family lived. One room of the building was reserved for the schoolroom. Here the children who met to study had no desks; the only furnishings of the room were benches made of rough tree slabs. But in spite of this poor equipment, little William and his school companions learned how to read, write, and do mathematical sums. Here they also memorized the catechism,[8] which was a part of their religious teaching.

But William was a student out-of-doors as well as in the schoolroom. He loved to read from the open book of nature, for he loved

---

[8] A book summarizing the basic principles of Christianity in question-and-answer form. From the Greek: katēkhismos: to teach by word of mouth.

plant life and the wild little insects and birds that lived in the open spaces. He enjoyed going on hikes through the woodlands which bordered the village and down the dusty lanes or across the meadows, in search of wild flowers, insects, or birds. His mother, understanding his love of nature, permitted him to stock his bedroom with a collection of curios[9] dear to his boy-heart. By closely watching them he early learned the habits of the birds, insects, and plants which he studied. While still a boy, he was recognized as the best informed person in the village on natural history, for when anyone discovered an unusual bird, insect, or flower unknown to the other villagers, they would say, "Tek it to Bill Carey; he'll tell you about it."

Because of his short stature William often had to climb trees in order to observe the habits of his out-of-door friends. One day, when climbing a difficult tree, he fell and injured himself. For several days he suffered from the injuries and had to stay in bed, but almost the first thing he did as soon as he was able to get about again was to tackle that same tree and climb it successfully. He was a lad who believed "I can." If he failed the first time, he kept on trying again and again until he did what he set out to do.

As a boy William did not spend all of his

---

[9] Curious or unusual objects, perhaps worth collecting.

time in the schoolroom or at play. He was the eldest child in the family and the first one to help share the family burdens. He carried water from the spring down the lane at the foot of the hill, and he brought firewood from the forest outside the village. These tasks led him along nature's trails where he used to keep his eyes open to learn her secrets. Sometimes he would take his little sister along to show her a rare plant that he had found, or to gather wild flowers.

William was quite young when his hero-uncle, Peter Carey, returned to the village after an absence of many years. He had been soldiering in the new world, America, and many thrilling tales he told about Canada's Indians, about the war with the French and the capture of Quebec, and about his adventures on the stormy sea. Listening to these tales, William felt a longing to learn more about lands across the seas and of strange peoples. Already he had begun to reveal an interest in the study of other languages, memorizing pages and pages of foreign words.

Books were not so numerous in that long ago time when William was a lad; the few he read were of scientific interest or of human interest adventures in travel. He talked so much of Columbus, the discoverer of America, that his companions nicknamed him after his hero.

While actual happenings interested him more than make-believe stories, still the adventures of Robinson Crusoe held for him the same fascination which has thrilled boy-readers from his generation down to the present time.

Not that William was always studying when he was a lad. In the lively game of "Stagastaroney" which the village children played, he was chosen to be *it* as often as were the other boys. And then he chased the others until, aided by his captives, he caught the entire group. Years later, in far-away India, how well he followed the principles of this childhood game in his great life-work!

The schoolroom door swung shut behind William for the last time when he was only twelve, for he had finished the grades in the village school, and his parents were too poor to send him away to continue his studies elsewhere. The time had come when he must begin to work for a livelihood and prepare to be a man. But this did not mean for William that he ceased to study; whenever he had a spare moment and a good book to read, he sought to add to his store of knowledge. And because he thus faithfully made the most of his opportunities, he was ready to become a college professor when India's first college needed such a man.

But William did not think about ever

becoming a college professor when he left the schoolroom of his boyhood. He planned to become a field-tiller, or gardener, like his hero-uncle, Peter. He loved plant-life and was eager to cultivate the fields and raise food products. For two years he followed the plow along the furrows and watched the growth of his garden. But during those years he suffered so much from sunburn that he could hardly sleep at night, and finally his father decided to train him for other work. So he let him work for a shoemaker who lived in a neighboring village.

William was expected to work for seven years in this shoemaker's employ, learning the trade. Young lads were often placed in shops like that to learn trades, and they were called apprentices. Another and older lad named John Warr was also working for William's employer, and the boys spent much time together. John was a kind, thoughtful lad, and he took time to help William learn shoecraft. He also helped his young friend to find Jesus as his personal Savior, and this proved to be the greatest and happiest discovery of William's lifetime.

In his spare moments, William used to examine the books on his master's shelf. One day he found in a New Testament commentary some strange letters which he supposed must certainly represent another language. But no one about the shop could explain their meaning to him. Determined to find out, William copied them with great care and took them home on his next visit to Paulers Pury. There he found a man whom he knew had once been a student of ancient languages. Showing the letters to him, he asked, "Do you know what languages these letters represent?"

"Yes," replied the man, "that is Greek." Then the man gave William his first lesson in Greek. William also studied Latin, Hebrew, Italian, and Dutch, and learned how to use these languages. All of this he did while working as a shoe cobbler in a plain little shop.

When William grew to manhood he continued his work as a shoe cobbler, but he also began to preach the gospel to the people in the village where he lived. Sometimes he visited other villages and preached there also. During these years he began to think a great deal about the people who live in countries where the true God is not known. He believed that they, too, should be taught about God. He began to study the geographical location of other countries, and finally he drew a large map of the world, which he hung on the walls of his workshop. Every day as he cobbled shoes that map hung before him, reminding him of the millions of people who were dying without a knowledge of the Savior, Jesus Christ.

Not only did William think a great deal about the neglected heathen, he also talked about them. Other ministers at that time believed that the "notion" of trying to convert the heathen was foolish. But finally some of them began to understand that William was right. They began to believe, too, that God expected them to take the gospel to the people of every nation. William said he would go as a missionary if the church would send him. For several years he waited, hoping to go to the islands in the South Pacific. During those years he kept busy working as a shoe cobbler to support his family, studying languages, and preaching the gospel on Sundays.

At last a call came for someone to go to India to begin missionary work there. William Carey was ready to answer that call. Taking his wife and four children, he sailed away from England on June 13, 1793. For five months they sailed and sailed; sailing vessels did not make fast time, and besides, they had to sail around the southernmost cape of Africa—there was no shorter water route to India in that century.

When at last they reached India, William Carey found that his first task would be to learn the language of the people before he could tell them about the true God and the way of salvation. So he set to work to study the principal language of that part of India where they were located. This language is called Bengali. He soon found that different languages are spoken in different parts of the country, and that he would need to know several languages if he wished to travel about and preach the gospel. As soon as he learned Bengali well enough to understand its meaning, he began to write the Bible, word for word, in that language. What a task this was! But he kept faithfully at it until the last verse was translated from English into Bengali.

When William was ready to print the first Bible in the language of India, he found out that much money would be needed to do this work. He had none, but he did not give up hope. Soon a friend, knowing his desire, gave him a printing-press. How happy he and his helpers were to set it up and learn how to use it! They worked so earnestly at the press that some of their Bengali neighbors, looking on, thought the press was their idol. Little did those idol-worshippers realize that the hand-press was going to help break down idol-worship in India.

After living in India only seven years, William could speak the Bengali language so fluently that he was asked to teach the language in the first college founded in that country. He and his Indian helpers had to write a Bengali grammar and other textbooks to use in the college. During this time he kept on studying other Indian languages also, and soon he was teaching three of them to the college students.

Not only did William Carey study languages and teach in the college at Calcutta and preach the gospel to groups of listening heathen, he also found time to work in a garden near his home. Here he spent many happy hours among his flowers and plants. He also watched the birds and insects of that country and studied their habits. This out-of-door occupation benefited his health and made him stronger for his indoor work. We are told that many plants found throughout the district of Bengal today came from seeds that had been scattered by the wind or carried by the birds from William Carey's garden. And many visitors from other lands were delighted to walk through the garden of this first missionary, whose love of nature continued as long as he lived.

Although William Carey taught in the college for many years and worked in his garden nearly every day, he kept his mind on the great need which had brought him away from his homeland to a heathen country. Year after year he worked at the great task which he had first set out to do. That task was giving to the people of India the Bible in their own tongue. There were so many languages to master that any other person would have been discouraged.

But William never gave up. Finally he had the joy of seeing the whole Bible printed in six different languages as a result of his hard work. Then he kept on, and by and by he had translated the New Testament and part of the Old Testament into five more languages, the entire New Testament into eighteen other languages, and the Gospels into five others, making thirty-four languages into which he had written the whole or parts of the Bible. What a wonderful work for one man to accomplish!

Besides giving the Bible to millions of India's people, William Carey also had the joy of giving his three sons as missionaries to the heathen. They grew up to love the work which had called their father away from his home country to a strange, unfriendly people, for they shared the same beautiful Christian spirit which made their father's life such a blessing in the world.

After spending forty-one years—more than one-half of his lifetime—in India, William Carey ceased his labors and died in that land. But not until he had made the work far easier for other missionaries who would follow him to that country to tell the gospel story, for they would find the Bible already waiting in the languages of the people.

CHAPTER X

The Boy Who Asked Puzzling Questions.

IT was springtime in Milan, Ohio, and the Edisons were planning to raise geese, so they set an old goose in the usual fashion, hoping that she would hatch a flock of goslings. Little Al, their six-year-old, watched them place the eggs in the nest, and many were the questions he asked about how those eggs would be changed into "baby geese." The answers to his questions proved so unsatisfactory that he decided to find out the truth for himself; so quietly he began to collect and carry food to the vicinity of the nest, then he chased off the old goose and stationed himself on the nest in her stead. His intention was "to see how it was done," and he had made provisions to remain at his post until the experiment was given a fair trial. How bitter, then, must have been his disappointment when his amazed parents found him sitting there and broke up his plan!

Little Al was always asking puzzling questions. Sometimes his father, annoyed by them, would be compelled to admit that he did not know how to answer them correctly. Then the child would ask quite innocently, "Why don't you know?"

From a goose nest into a great laboratory is a long jump, but the little lad who spread his dress skirt over the goose eggs to keep them warm (six-year-old boys wore dresses in 1853) grew into the man whose wonderful inventions have brought him world-wide fame.

Strange as it may seem, many folk thought that little Al was lacking somewhat in ordinary intelligence because he asked so many questions, which they considered foolish. When only a little boy he used to feel that his father thought him rather stupid, and sometimes he wondered whether he really was a dunce. Especially after his parents moved from Milan, Ohio (where he had been born on February 11, 1847) to Port Huron, Michigan, and entered him in the Huron public school, did this matter trouble him. For in spite of his seven years, he could not advance in his class, and at the end of three months he overheard the teacher tell the school inspector that it would not be worthwhile keeping him in school any longer. A heartbroken little boy, he rushed home to his mother that day to tell her what he had heard. Until this time he had kept his fears to himself, for he knew his mother believed in him and he could not bear the thought of her finding out that he was really dull. But now he knew she would find out, so he resolved to be the first to tell her the sad story.

Mrs. Edison was a real mother. Of course she believed in her boy. She knew he was not stupid. She knew he could learn. She had been a school-teacher before she married Mr. Edison, and she understood boys. So she comforted her small son and assured him that she would help him learn. From that time he did not re-enter the public schools but studied faithfully at home, with his mother as instructor, and quickly learned how to read, write, and do sums. He made rapid progress in the elementary grades, and at the age of nine he was beginning to manifest an interest in electricity and science. Directed by his mother, he read several historical books before he was twelve years old. His interest in electricity and science continued to grow, and he eagerly read up on these subjects. When he came to difficult or uninteresting chapters in these books, he did not skip over them but asked his mother to explain their meaning to him. Years later when he became a famous inventor he said, "My mother was the making of me. She was so true, so sure of me; I felt that I had someone to live for, someone I must not disappoint. I did not have my mother very long, but in that length of time she cast over me an influence which has lasted all my life. The good effect of her early training I can never lose. If it had not been for her appreciation and her faith in me at a critical time in my experiences, I should very likely never have become an inventor."

When about eleven years old, Al grew restless in the "home schoolroom" and wanted to get some kind of job and go to work. But his mother did not approve of the plan, for she thought he was too young to become a wage-earner for the family. After some time, however, he won her over to his way of thinking, and then he applied for the position of newsboy on the train which ran between his home town and Detroit. While waiting for his application to be approved, he sold newspapers on the street, for he believed then, as he does now,[10] that it does not matter much what kind of work one does so long as the work is honest.

While peddling his wares on the train, Al became acquainted with the railroad men—the

---

[10] Edison was still alive when this book was first printed in 1931.

engineers, conductors, and depot agents. He heard them exchange news items at various stops, and finally the thought occurred to him to print a special news sheet for their benefit. Although he had never worked in a printing office, he believed he could print such a paper. So he bought a second-hand press and some type, learned how to set it up, and got to work. Then he put the machinery in an unused compartment of the mail car and began to edit the first newspaper printed on a moving train. He called his paper the *Weekly Herald*, and by keeping his eyes and ears open he collected enough items to fill the columns of his paper every week. He sold single copies for three cents each, or monthly subscriptions for eight cents. His subscription list grew to five hundred, and besides that number he printed two hundred extra copies to be sold on the train. In four years he had earned two thousand dollars, all of which he gave to his parents.

But Al was not content to do the same work day after day; he wished to learn how to do other things, too. So he hired other boys to assist him, and while they carried his wares through the coaches he remained in his "printing office," experimenting with telegraphy and chemicals. One day while he was experimenting, the train ran over a rough bit of track and gave a heavy lurch which tossed a bottle of phosphorous to the floor. In dismay Al saw flames leap up and catch on the woodwork of the car. He fought to smother them but was making poor headway when the conductor entered the car and came to his assistance. In a little while they put the fire out; then the conductor turned to young Al and gave him a severe scolding. He also boxed the boy's ears so severely that the hearing was destroyed in one of them. Then as the train slowed up at the Mt. Clemens station, he flung the door open and threw all of Al's belongings out onto the platform in a broken heap. Al went with them, and never again did he edit his *Weekly Herald* on the train. Rather a battered-up, bewildered boy he must have been as he stood there on the platform, looking at the wreck of his belongings while the train moved on.

But Al did not belong to the class of quitters. He stuck to his task of selling papers, magazines, candy, peanuts, and other miscellaneous articles on the train for some time. He set up his printing headquarters at home, however, and kept his experimenting material out of the conductor's reach.

One day, when he was stopping off at Mt. Clemens chatting with the agent, he saw Jimmy, the agent's two-year-old son, toddle off the platform into the middle of a track just as a heavy freight train was approaching. Seeing the danger, Al leaped forward and caught the child from under the wheels of the engine. The grateful father, being a telegraph operator, promised as a reward to teach Al how to receive and send messages over the wire. This was much to Al's liking. So for the next three months he stopped off at Mt. Clemens four evenings each week on his home run to study telegraphy, and at the end of that time he had learned all the station agent could teach. Then he applied for the position of night operator at his home town, and in spite of his youth, he was accepted.

The fifteen-year-old night operator was so eager to continue his experiments in the daytime that he could not always keep awake when on duty, and finally he lost his job at the Port Huron station. His next position he also lost as a result of experimenting when he should have been attending to his duties in the office. His inquiring mind continued to lead him on, and all the while he kept up his experiments, learning more and more until finally, plans for inventions began to take shape in his thoughts. If only he had money to work them out! But he was always short of funds, for he invested heavily in second-hand books and in materials to experiment with, besides sending money home regularly to his parents. He continued to be a great reader of scientific books and magazines and lived as cheaply as possible in order to keep well supplied with these. One day he bought at an auction a very large pile of *North American Reviews* for two dollars, and while taking them home from the office where he worked until three o'clock in the morning he was mistaken for a thief by a policeman. Failing to hear the officer's command to halt because of his deafness, Al was suddenly made aware of the fact that he was in danger when a bullet whizzed past his head. "If I had been a better shot," said the officer, "you would have been killed."

While in Boston during his early twenties, Al took out his first patent for an invention. But the invention proved disappointing, and he resolved thereafter never to invent anything which the majority of people could not appreciate. He worked nights in the Western Union Telegraph Company's office, and slept but little during the day, spending most of the time in the public library, second-hand book shops, and his laboratory. Returning from his work one morning at three o'clock, he brought a set of books on electricity and read eagerly until time to go for breakfast. His mind was so filled with fresh enthusiasm from what he had read that he suddenly exclaimed to his companion and roommate, "Adams, I've got so much to do, and life is so short, that I am going to hustle." And with that he started on a dead run down the street to a restaurant after his breakfast.

The time came when Al felt that he must have a laboratory of his own, so he left Boston and went to New York City to look for work. For several nights he slept on a park bench, and one day he had nothing to eat. One morning he stepped into the office of the Gold and Stock Indicator Company on Wall Street. The stock indicator, or ticker, had stopped, and the repairmen seemed unable to locate the trouble. "I think I can fix it," said Al to the owner, and in a very short time he had it working again. The owner was well pleased and offered to pay him three hundred dollars a month if he would keep the ticker going. To Al the offer seemed amazingly good, but he calmly replied that he would not accept the position unless a part of the first month's pay was advanced to him "in good faith." He really did not want it for "good faith" but for food, as he had gone without anything to eat for nearly thirty hours.

Al soon discovered that the ticker was very unreliable, so he set his wits to work at the task of making it a trustworthy instrument. Finally he succeeded, and the president of the company asked what he would take for his work. He thought of asking five thousand dollars but decided to let the company make the first offer, and when the president mentioned forty thousand dollars, like a wise man he quietly accepted that amount.

The time had come at last when young Edison could have a laboratory of his very own. And that he has made good use of it during the years which have followed all the world knows, for his untiring labors in his laboratory have resulted in the invention of many great things. The electric lights which brighten our homes were made possible by his spending thirteen months of tireless labor in experimenting. When one thing failed he would try another, and still another, until he found the thing needed to make his experiment a success. Also our phonographs, moving pictures, speaking parts of the telephone, appliances for use on electric railways, storage batteries, and ever so many other things we owe to the untiring labor of this truly great man.

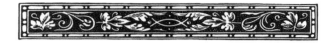

CHAPTER XI

The Lad Whose Fame Grew In A Garden.

IN a large, brick farmhouse, set some distance back from the road that led to the village of Lancaster, Massachusetts, lived the happy Burbank family. Already there were twelve boys and girls in that household when on March 7, 1849, a baby brother was born who was destined to become famous.

Near the farmhouse was a flower garden, the especial pride of Mrs. Burbank. When baby Luther grew old enough to toddle about, she used to take him with her into the garden to admire the pretty blossoms. Never did he tear their brightly colored petals apart as babies do, but if a petal fell he would try earnestly to replace it. One day he saw a hummingbird sipping nectar from the fuchsia of a beautiful blossom. Thinking the bird would destroy the flower, he caught it in his baby fingers and ran to his mother crying, "Birdie eat flower! Birdie eat flower!" But when his mother explained that the bird was only taking food from the flowers which nature had placed there for its use, he quickly released it. And afterwards he enjoyed watching the bees, butterflies, and humming birds flit about from flower to flower, gathering food and making themselves very much at home among the blossoms.

One of Luther's odd playthings when he was a wee child was a lobster cactus in a pot. This he used to carry about as a child would a doll. One day while carrying it he stumbled and fell, breaking the pot and the plant, and almost breaking his heart. How well he recalled the incident when he grew to manhood we do not know, but long afterwards, when he had established for himself a world-wide reputation as a naturalist, he spent ten years developing from the wild desert cactus a plant without spines or "prickles," which makes excellent food for cattle.

Luther seemed to prefer plants to other children as playmates. He loved not only the well-cultivated flowers which bloomed profusely in his mother's garden, but the wayside buttercups, the nodding goldenrods, and the plain little field daisies too. He felt grieved to hear the daisies called a pest and resolved that someday he would teach them how to become beautiful, respectable flowers that people would welcome in their gardens. And sure enough, one of his achievements has been the cultivation of the common field daisy into a garden flower, the Shasta daisy.

Early in the springtime, Luther used to be right on hand when the dry, lifeless-looking bulbs were brought out from the cellar and placed in the earth. Then he would watch for the first tiny green shoots as they sprang up to greet the sunshine and continue his observations until the flower stalks bloomed forth in iris, golden daffodil, and scarlet tulip.

But flowers were not the only plants that claimed Luther's attention and interest. The vegetable garden also opened some fascinating pages in nature's wonder book. Here as a farmer lad he pulled weeds and hoed corn just as farmer lads do today. But along with the tiresome work he found pleasure in watching the wonderful moving picture that the growing plant life presented. When seed-gathering time came, he noticed that always seeds were selected from the first large, ripe tomato, the finest melon, the most perfect ear of corn—always from the best of everything. Thus as a boy he learned the first great principle of all plant improvement—the principle of selection. Then the seed-planting season was another event of interest to young Luther. He learned that some seeds are sown directly in the earth while others must first be cared for in the hot-beds or boxes made for that purpose and later transplanted in the soil when the warm sunshine has taken the frost out of the ground.

Boylike, Luther sometimes mixed play with his work. When the early lettuce peeped out of the ground and the bright green letters spelling L-u-t-h-e-r, one did not need to guess who had sown the lettuce seed. When a large cucumber was found hidden among the leaves in a glass bottle having such a narrow neck that it barely admitted the slender vine, no one was at a loss to know who had placed the tiny cucumber in the glass prison to watch its development day after day. And when the initials "L.B." were found traced with the point of a penknife on little pumpkins, Luther was merely wanting to see those letters increase in size as the pumpkins grew larger. Once, after having watched a circus parade pass by, Luther traced on the little pumpkins outlines of elephants, lions, tigers, and other circus symbols, and when those same pumpkins grew up they were taken to the county fair and put on display, causing much merriment to the beholders.

Luther Burbank's first teacher in the district school not far from his home was his elder brother, Herbert. Sometimes when the snow was too deep for his little feet, Herbert would draw Luther to school on his hand sled. At school Luther was a shy, sensitive little boy, too timid to enjoy the fun and laughter of the other children. But as he grew older, he became the leader in the little band of barefoot boys who searched through the meadow and woodland pasture for nature's treasured store of nuts and wild fruits. He knew where the sweetest strawberries hid in the meadow grasses, where the biggest blueberries grew in the woodland pasture, and just where to find the best chestnuts and hickory nuts.

Luther used to examine the tiny mosses and lichens that grew on old stone walls and wished that he might study them with the aid of a magnifying glass. When he grew old enough to earn money for himself, one of the first things which he purchased with his own earnings was a microscope. Then he found great delight in studying nature and discovering beauty in flowers and mosses that is hidden from the unaided eye. He liked to read books on science and compare the facts gleaned from books with the facts which he learned in nature's schoolroom.

At the age of fifteen, Luther enrolled as

a student at the Lancaster Academy, where he continued his studies for several winters. He walked to school each day a distance of three miles and often retraced his steps in the evening to enjoy an hour's practice in the gymnasium. During the summer months, he worked in Worcester learning the mechanic's trade. Although he much preferred to be an out-of-door workman, soiling his hands with earth rather than with the grease of a mechanic's shop, he did faithful work in Worcester. He paid close attention to the machinery in the shop, and one day he thought of an improvement which would mean a great deal to his employer. So he carefully worked out a model and presented it to his employer, who was pleased with the suggestion and offered to increase Luther's salary. How surprised the man must have been when Luther quietly refused the offer and explained that he was going back to the farm to do the kind of work he liked best!

One does not become a great naturalist all at once; much is to be learned and great patience is required to try out experiments. But Luther Burbank's first great experiment in plant growing made him famous, even though he was still a very young man. He had read an article in the county newspaper concerning the inferior quality o⁶ the potatoes then raised, and the thought occurred to his mind to begin his experiments with the potato. So when he found a seed ball on one of his potato plants, he decided to watch carefully until the seeds would be ready to leave the mother plant. Then, after his diligence, at the last moment he feared he had lost the treasure, for when he went to gather the seed, the ball had disappeared. By careful searching, however, he found it some distance from the vine, unharmed. From that seed ball he took twenty-six tiny seeds so small that ten of them were not as large as an ordinary pinhead. These he saved until the following spring; then he planted them and waited through the long summer for the vines and the potatoes to grow in each hill. He took those from one hill to the agricultural fair held in the neighborhood, and there he met one of the greatest seedsmen of the United States, who became attracted to his experiment. He urged Luther to continue testing those new potatoes and promised that if they proved as good as they looked, he would buy them. After three years of further testing, Luther sent the potatoes to the seedsman and received one hundred dollars for his new product. The seedsman christened the potato "Burbank" in honor of its originator, and since that time more than five hundred million bushels of Burbank potatoes have been raised from that one tiny seed. Because they withstand the blight better than other varieties of potatoes, they were introduced into Ireland, the great potato-growing country, and hailed with delight by the Irish peasants, who depend upon tubers as one of their principal foods.

Not long after those first successful experiments, Luther Burbank decided to leave his home in Massachusetts and go to a warmer climate to continue his work. So he crossed the continent to California and located at Santa Rosa. Here he took sick and soon was forced to spend all his money for the bare necessities of life. For a while he was glad to seek refuge in an empty chicken-house and work at whatever odd jobs he could get. But he continued to be hopeful, and slowly he regained his health until finally he was able to earn enough money to buy some land and begin again the work that he loved the best.

More than fifty years have passed since Luther Burbank created a rare garden spot in his southern California home, and during those years wonderful things have taken place in that garden. Strange plants have come to that garden from the garden of the king of Italy, others from the gardens of Japan, and still others from far-away Siberia, India, Australia, Patagonia, Alaska, New Zealand,

China, and South America. These plants have been brought to be educated and trained to gain new habits and qualities that will make them of greater worth to the world.

Under the watchful eye and patient skill of their great teacher, Luther Burbank, some of the flowers have been induced to change the color of their dresses; some have been persuaded to drop their bad habits; others have developed sweet perfumes. He has trained sour fruits to become sweet; good-for-nothing berries to become edible; and from bitter nuts he has extracted the puckery nature. Millions of plants—grasses, flowers, vegetables, grains, and trees—have passed through his hands, and from these he has selected a few to develop to such a point that they may become the most pleasing as food, or beautiful as ornaments, or useful for the service of mankind.

No wonder people called the man who accomplished so many unheard-of wonders in the vegetable kingdom the "Plant Wizard." But to those who knew him best, Luther Burbank was always a sincere, modest, ever busy man with a great mission to fulfill on earth and with a great desire to fulfill it rightly. And the succeeding generations of the human race will continue in debt to this faithful toiler whose skill has beautified their gardens, improved the flavor and selling qualities of their fruits, and rendered their vegetables more toothsome and abundant. Of him it has been aptly written:

He walked with Patience
many a tedious hour;
With Genius' glowing lamp
aflame in hand;
Or sat with her in Wisdom's citadel,
And heard the watchman calling,
'All is well';
Then saw the shrunken,
blighted bloom expand
Into a graceful, snowy,
starry flower.

CHAPTER XII

THE LAD WHO WAS
CONQUERED BY LOVE.

ONE November evening, two boys wandered down the main street of a New England village and stopped in front of a hardware store to view the articles on display in the window. The younger of them, a little fellow only eight years old, had been crying. In spite of his brother's earnest effort to fix his attention on some attractive object in the window, Dwight continued to sniffle. What did he care about jackknives or marbles or baseballs when his heart was breaking with homesickness?

That very morning those two boys had kissed their widowed mother good-by and had walked away from their home, thirteen miles distant, to live in the village during the winter and attend school there. They could earn their boards and lodging by doing chores and running errands outside of school hours. But Dwight had never been so far from home before, nor had he ever been quite so unhappy. His brother had spent several weeks in the village and was somewhat acquainted with the village folk.

Just then an old man came tottering down the street toward them, and Dwight's brother said, "Here comes a man who will give you a cent."

"How do you know?" asked Dwight, doubtfully.

"Because he gives a cent to every new boy who comes to town."

That sounded reasonable, so Dwight made a brave effort to hide his tears and strode out into the middle of the sidewalk where the old man would be sure to see him. When the man approached, he stopped and said, "This is a new boy in town, isn't it?"

"Yes sir," replied Dwight's brother, politely; "he just came today."

Dwight expected to see him put his hand into his pocket at once and take out a cent, but instead of doing that the old man took off Dwight's cap and placed his trembling hand on the small boy's head. He talked to the boys and learned why they had come to the village. Then looked into Dwight's tear-washed eyes and told him about the heavenly Father who loved him. Dwight felt that the old man really cared for him, and he listened quietly to his quavering voice, almost forgetting about the expected cent. But presently the stranger reached into his pocket and took out a brand new copper that looked just like gold and gave it to him. Then he passed on.

To Dwight that small copper seemed like a fortune. He had never known the joyous expectancy that other boys feel when they see their fathers thrust their hands down deep into their trousers pockets to bring up the equivalent of a bag of candy or an ice-cream cone. His father had died when he was only a four-year-old, and his mother had needed every penny, nickel, and dime to feed and clothe her family of seven boys and two girls. No wonder he treasured that cent! But long after the treasure parted company with its youthful owner, Dwight remembered the kind words with which the old man had eased his heartache that night.

Dwight's father had died suddenly, leaving many debts and no money with which to pay them. Even the home in which the family lived was mortgaged, but the law of the State preserved it for the widow and her children. Soon the creditors came and took away everything they could lay their hands on, even the kindling wood. One cold morning Mrs. Moody kept the children in bed until time to go to school because she had no wood to build a fire. But Dwight's Uncle Cyrus came to their rescue that very morning, bringing a load of wood and cutting it into stove-lengths. More than once that kind-hearted man helped the struggling widow through the first long year after her husband died, while other people wagged their heads and predicted that she could never keep her family together and rear them to respectable manhood and womanhood. But years later, when Mrs. Moody died in that same community, she had thoroughly convinced every doubter that a good mother is not a quitter.

Dwight, her fifth child, was born on her birthday, February 5, 1837. In spite of the poverty which hung like a dark shadow over their home, Dwight and his brothers and sisters were fun-loving, home-loving children, for their mother contrived to make their home attractive. Although the older boys hired out to the farmers near Northfield, Massachusetts, their home town, during the summer months they always came home on Saturday evenings to spend Sunday with their mother, brothers, and sisters. Thus Mrs. Moody kept the family reunited one day out of seven while the boys and girls were growing up.

And Sundays were never-to-be-forgotten days for the Moody household, beginning as they always did with sunset on Saturday evening. Then a quiet reverence settled over the home and lingered until sunset on the following day. The family attended Sunday school and church services regularly, walking the distance of one mile. The boys used to go barefoot, carrying their stockings and shoes in their hands until they came in sight of the church, then stopped to put them on. Nor did they ever argue the question with their mother whether or not they would attend services at the church, for Mrs. Moody's word was law and woe befell the child who dared to disregard it. After Dwight grew to manhood, he often praised his mother for having so faithfully instilled into her children the church-going habit. For a time, when he could not understand the minister's sermons, he used to feel peeved[11] because he had to go to church, but later when he grew into young manhood and went away from home, he found that the habit had become so fixed he did not care to break it.

Dwight's first experience as a wage-earner

---

[11] Irritated; annoyed.

came one summer when he took the neighbor's cows out to pasture on a mountain near by, receiving one cent a day for his labor. When he was eight years old, he hired out with an elder brother to cut broom corn for a farmer who lived across the river from their home. But more often he hired out during the winter months to do chores and thus earn his board and lodging while going to school.

A stern, quick-tempered schoolmaster took most of the joy out of the schooling that Dwight received, for unfortunately for Dwight, his love of learning did not always keep pace with his love of fun, and as a consequence he received numerous floggings. But finally a new teacher came into the schoolroom—a woman. The boys expected to have a gay[12] time, and Dwight, their leader, felt sure that his days of suffering from the application of the teacher's rod were at an end, for the new teacher announced the fact that she expected to rule the school by love! When on the first morning she opened the day's program with prayer, asking God to give her grace and strength to rule wisely, a hush fell over the scholars, akin to reverence. They had never seen the like of that and felt awed by such unusual proceedings. But after several days the newness began to wear off and Dwight found himself the first violator

[12] Merry; lively; happy; joyful; light-hearted.

of the schoolroom discipline. When the new teacher requested him to remain after school, he stiffened himself into the expectant attitude of a school culprit awaiting his fate. But much to his surprise she did not attempt to punish him. Instead she sat down beside him and talked quietly and earnestly until he felt ashamed and penitent.[13] He promised to obey the rules thereafter, and never again did he disappoint her by causing trouble in the schoolroom, although he was a fun-loving boy.

One lesson that Mrs. Moody taught her children was the importance of keeping a promise. When once they agreed to do a certain thing, she held them to do it. She never asked, "Can you do it?" but rather, "Did you say that you would?" One winter Dwight had agreed to work for a neighbor for board while attending school, but after spending some time there, he came home complaining that for nineteen meals his only food had been corn meal and milk with occasional crusts of bread too hard for the family to eat. His mother asked if enough food was set before him to satisfy his hunger, and when she learned that he had had plenty to eat, such as it was, she sent him back to keep his agreement. No wonder Dwight was careful about making promises all his lifetime, after that!

---

[13] Sorrow or remorse for wrongdoing.

At the age of seventeen, Dwight Moody went to Boston to find work. He had an uncle living in that city that he hoped would offer him a place in his shoe-store. But he was disappointed. After searching elsewhere and finding no one willing to hire him, he came to his uncle one day and asked for work. His uncle feared that he might not become a successful salesman, but wishing to encourage Dwight he told him that he would hire him if he would promise to take advice and to attend Sunday school and church services regularly. This Dwight promised to do, and in a short time he surprised his uncle by becoming the best salesman in his employ.

Dwight had not been in Boston long when one day the gentleman who taught his class at Sunday school came into the store to talk to him about becoming a Christian. As a result of that talk Dwight was persuaded to give his heart to God. At once he felt a desire to work for his new Master, but because he did not know how to express his love for God very clearly, the older Christians to whom he talked did not think he was prepared to do Christian work. He did not grow discouraged and cease trying to do right because they refused to give him something to do in their church, but kept on living a clean, pure life.

When Dwight L. Moody was still a very young man he left Boston and went to Chicago to find work. He hoped to make a great deal of money and some day become a very rich man. Here he found work again in a shoe-store and continued to be a salesman. He worked faithfully and his employer quickly learned that he was a Christian and could be trusted. He also found out that Dwight was busy all the time he was awake, for on Sundays he attended church, taking with him the young men whom he could persuade to leave the streets and go into a house of worship. At the church where he attended services, he reserved four pews which he planned to fill with young men who did not attend services anywhere.

One Sunday afternoon Dwight visited a mission Sunday school where the poorer people attended services. He told the superintendent that he would like to teach a class, but the superintendent replied that already he had more persons wishing to be teachers than pupils to be taught. "If you will bring scholars for a class, you may teach," the superintendent said. The next Sunday Dwight returned with eighteen ragged boys whom he had gathered from the streets. He did not keep the class for himself, but volunteered to go out and find other scholars, and soon there was a thriving Sunday school.

Not long afterwards, Dwight visited another part of Chicago where there were no churches but plenty of saloons and other places of wickedness. He decided that would be the very place to begin a Sunday school, so he secured a hall and began to gather in the neglected children who had never been taught about the love of God. His Sunday school grew until the place was filled, and then the school was moved to a larger building. The enrollment reached one thousand, and although many of the children were rough and ragged when Dwight first brought them into his Sunday school, some of them grew up to be respectable citizens of which Chicago felt proud.

As a drawing-card to attract and hold the boys and girls in the Sunday school, this remarkable man used kindness. Many of these children came from homes where there were drunken fathers and mothers and where kindness was unknown. Dwight visited such homes and persuaded many of those parents to become Christians. Finally, his Sunday school grew into a community church, and Dwight grew into a preacher of the gospel.

Not long afterwards the world began to hear about this earnest preacher, and Dwight L. Moody was invited to other great cities of America to hold revivals. He crossed the Atlantic Ocean to Great Britain twice to conduct revivals in the British Isles, and wherever he went, thousands of people flocked to hear him. But always he remained the same humble, earnest Christian man who started his work for God in the slums of Chicago, bringing the neglected children into Sunday school.

For more than forty years this wonderful man engaged in Christian work, helping millions of people by bringing to them the glad news of salvation. So diligently did he study, teach, and preach that finally he wore himself out. In December of 1899 he returned to his home near Northfield, Massachusetts, and there he died soon afterwards as triumphantly as he had lived.

CHAPTER XIII

The Boy Who Discovered
That Wire Can "Talk."

WHAT a long, long time the world stood before the people living in it discovered that their voices could be heard plainly by persons at a distance and out of sight! Then came the marvelous invention of a device called the telephone, and people wagged their heads, exclaiming, "That new-fangled thing will never amount to much. It is only a toy." More years passed by; and now great continents are crossed from shore to shore by wires which make possible the carrying of the human voice for thousands of miles, to be heard and clearly understood by a loved one, a friend, or a business associate. And so the telephone has become one of the marvels of the age in which we live.

Because the telephone has come to fill such an important part in the daily program of business and in the social interest of the world, humanity owes a debt of gratitude to the man who invented it. As a tribute to his honor, the great system of telephony throughout our country bears his name; thus we have the "Bell Telephone Company," for to Alexander Graham Bell belongs the credit for the invention of this most serviceable instrument.

It is interesting to learn about the boyhood and early youth of this great man and to notice the influences which led him to render such great service to mankind.

Twenty-nine years before the birth of the telephone in the United States of America, little Alexander Graham Bell was born in the city of Edinburgh, Scotland, on March 3, 1847. His father was a lecturer on elocution[14] at the University of Edinburgh, and for a long time had been interested in the science of sound. His grandfather and an uncle had specialized in the study of the laws of speech and sound, and had taught and written on that subject. Doubtless little Alexander and his two brothers often heard them discuss their work. As they grew older these boys came to know about the

---

[14] Public speaking, including the control of voice and gesture.

system of "Visible Speech" which their father and grandfather had worked out, to be used in teaching correct speaking. The symbols used in this system were based upon the form and action of the vocal organs. By applying the rules of this system of "Visible Speech," persons who had been born deaf learned to talk. The Bell brothers soon found out that their father's work was very fascinating, and all three of them grew up to specialize in this same line of study.

As a boy Alexander attended school in Edinburgh, and at the age of fourteen he graduated from the Royal High School of that city. During this time he also studied music, his mother being his instructor at the piano. Because of his fondness for studying music, he added that knowledge to his study of the science of sound.

But Alexander was more than a student during his boyhood. He was very much an ordinary lad, as fond of fun and frolic as the rest of them. Sometimes he went out into the country to play near a grist-mill with the son of the miller. What fun they had scampering about on the banks of the mill-stream! One day the miller said, "Boys, I think you are growing big enough to learn how to do something useful."

"What can we do?" asked Alexander, meekly.

"You might help me remove the husks from this wheat," answered the busy man. So the two boys set to work at what proved to be quite a hard task. Their fingers were unused to such work, and the husks wore at the tender flesh.

Alexander wondered whether there would not be an easier way to remove the husks. "Why not use a small brush?" he reasoned. So he found one and tried it. Sure enough, the husks came off easier and he could do two or three times as much work. "So far, so good," thought young Alexander. "Why not put this wheat into the large rotary tank that is used in the mill, and let the paddle wheel throw it against brushes, or something rough like a brush?" He spoke to the miller who was pleased with the idea, so they tried the experiment and found that it worked well. This was Alexander's first experiment that proved beneficial to others.

But Alexander had no notion of becoming a miller when he grew up. Like all boys who greatly admire their fathers, he planned to follow his father's profession. As a little boy he used to play that he was a professor; when he grew older he still clung to that childhood fancy. One time he organized his friends into a club, which they called "The Society for the Promotion of Fine Arts among Boys." In this society every member could be a professor, and Alexander styled himself Professor of

Anatomy. He set about to make a collection of skeletons, animals, birds, etc., and his father encouraged him by giving suggestions and even by helping him collect objects for study. One time the young "professor" arranged to give a lecture on anatomy to a group of equally ambitious boys. He brought a dead little pig to dissect, and when he thrust a knife into the carcass, a groaning sound was emitted from its depths, caused by the sudden escape of some air that had remained in the animal. This unexpected sound threw the "professor" into a panic, and he was last seen on that occasion when he made a frightened exit through the door. Thereafter his interest in the society lost its fervor, and he turned his attention to other things.

Young Alexander carried on his experiments at home as well as when in company with his friends. He undertook the task of teaching his pet dog how to talk. Patiently he kept at it until he found out that by manipulating the dog's lower jaw the animal would make a noise that sounded like "Ow-ah-oo, ga-ma-ma." This, according to Alexander's interpretation, meant, "How are you, Grandmama?" Great was his delight when entertaining his friends to demonstrate before them this ability of his dog to talk.

After graduating from the Edinburgh high school, Alexander spent a year in London with his grandfather. While there he became more interested than ever in the science of sound, and although just a mere youth, he studied very seriously. His brothers were also specializing in this study and were preparing to teach. Before he was seventeen years old, he too applied for a position as a teacher in an academy at Elgin, Scotland, and was accepted. There his salary was fifty dollars a year and board, with instruction in Latin and Greek to fit him for the University. He must have proved himself a capable teacher and student, for later he enrolled at the Edinburgh University and in due time completed his work there and returned to Elgin Academy to become master and teacher of elocution and music.

Not long afterwards the Bell family bade farewell to their Scotland home and moved to London. Alexander wished to continue his studies, so he followed them to that city and enrolled at the University College and later at London University. During these years he became deeply interested in teaching deaf-born children how to speak, and before he was twenty-one he had successfully experimented with numbers of them. Because of this success he was chosen to carry on his father's work when the elder Bell left England for a lecturing tour in America.

Lamplighter

BUILDING CHARACTER
... ONE STORY AT A TIME

We would love to hear from you!

Please indicate the ages of readers in your family:

Preschool-7 yrs___   7-10___   10-13___   13-18___   18 and older___

☐ Send me information about your book clubs.

☐ Send me your FREE Lamplighter catalog, special offers,
and biblical insights email newsletter.

Name: _____

Address:_____

_____

Email: _____

Send to a friend:

Name: _____

Address:_____

_____

Email: _____

Call us toll-free at 1.888.246.7735
or visit WWW.LAMPLIGHTERPUBLISHING.COM

Lamplighter

PO BOX 777, WAVERLY, PA 18471

BUILDING CHARACTER
... ONE STORY AT A TIME

Another experiment now began to inter-est Alexander. He found that by using an electro-magnet he could produce vibrations on a tuning-fork which might lead him into scientific discovery. But he was hindered from carrying this experiment any further by illness which threatened his life.

Alexander's two brothers had both been stricken down and had died from tuberculo-sis, and now it seemed that he would develop the same weakness. So his parents decided to take him to another climate, hoping that the change would restore his health. Accordingly, they again bade good-by to their friends, and this time they sailed away across the Atlantic to America. Here they located near Brantford, Ontario, Canada, and much to their delight Alexander's health began to improve.

Near their new home lived a tribe of Mohawk Indians—the first red men of Alexander's acquaintance. He spent much time visiting them and teaching them the sign-language, called "Visible Speech," which his father had invented. Soon afterwards, the Board of Education of Boston, Massachusetts heard of his work and invited him to come to their city and teach in a school for deaf-mutes. Through his success in that school he won a professor-ship in Boston University.

Now Alexander's interests began to broaden

and include the mysteries of telegraphy. He knew that telegraph messages are carried by means of a charged wire, and he wondered why the human voice could not be carried on the wire. The more he thought about this idea the more reasonable it seemed to him. So he began to try to make an instrument that would send the voice over the wire and catch its clear tones at the other end.

Alexander realized that he could not make such an instrument by himself. He needed a helper who believed as he did, that the thing could be done. He needed someone who knew how to build all sorts of apparatus that inventors call for. And just such a man he found in his young friend, Thomas Watson, for Thomas was doing the kind of work Alexander's helper would have to know how to do. So Alexander told him about the new invention which he believed he could bring about with someone's help.

At first Thomas was too much surprised at the thought of such a new invention to know how to answer his friend. But finally he agreed to help Alexander, and the two young men set to work. They strung a wire through the house in which they were rooming, and at each end they attached a small instrument which Alexander had instructed Thomas to make. Then Thomas took his station in the basement, down three flights of stairs, and Alexander tried to talk to him. A sound came over the wire, which Thomas recognized as Alexander's voice, but he could not make out a word. This did not discourage the young men, for they knew they were on the right track. So they continued to work and work, trying to improve the instrument. Months passed by, and nearly a year, and then one day, while trying out their latest improvement, Thomas heard Alexander say, "Watson, come here, I want you." With a bound of delight Thomas sprang up the flights of stairs, and Alexander met him with a beaming face. At last they had succeeded.

So sure had they been of success that several weeks before this happened young Bell had applied to the patent office in Washington, D.C. for a patent securing his rights as inventor of the telephone, and on his twenty-ninth birthday the patent had arrived. One week later on March 10, 1876, the first distinct message was received over the wire.

At the Centennial Exposition, held in Philadelphia that year, the new invention was given its first public exhibition. People had come from all parts of the country and from distant lands to attend the Exposition and to view the wonderful development made in the United States of America during the previous one hundred years. One day the Emperor of

Brazil, Dom Pedro, was persuaded to listen over the telephone. Upon putting the receiver to his ear he exclaimed excitedly, "It talks!"

Then his friend, Lord Kelvin, who was an electrical scientist of the first rank and engineer of the Atlantic cable, also listened. "It does speak," he said. One after another the distinguished men in that group took their turn at the strange new instrument and were astonished to hear a human voice speaking over the wire. "This is the most remarkable thing I have seen in America," declared Lord Kelvin.

Although the telephone was highly praised by scientific men, other people were slow to realize its value. Even some businessmen declared it could never be a practical necessity, and Bell was ridiculed as "a crank who says he can talk through a wire." It seemed so absurd to think that one might speak into a tube or box-like instrument and be heard at a distance through a similar instrument at the other end of a wire. But a few warm friends of the young inventor encouraged him to keep right on, for they believed he had made a great discovery, which would be highly appreciated in the future. They furnished the money to continue his improvements and make the telephone a public benefit.

On the night of October 9, 1876, young Bell and his friend borrowed the use of the telegraph wire between Boston and Cambridge, attached their instruments at each end, and carried on the first long distance conversation in the country, over a distance of two miles. Almost forty years later they used the same instruments and spoke over four thousand miles of wire, from San Francisco to New York. By that time the telephone had gained popularity, until it was considered most important to the interest of the public in all civilized lands.

When the world woke up to the value of this marvelous invention, Alexander Graham Bell was not without honor. From the Land of the Rising Sun, the Emperor bestowed on him the highest gift of recognition; from the Royal Society of Great Britain and Society of Fine Arts of London he received medals; while the Government of France made him an officer of the Legion of Honor and awarded him the Volta prize of fifty thousand francs. This money he used when he founded the Volta Bureau in Washington "for the increase and diffusing knowledge relating to the deaf." Never did he cease his interest in behalf of the deaf, although he devoted much of his time in later years to other research for the benefit of mankind. In a sense, the world owes to the deaf the invention of the telephone, for had Bell not studied every phase of sound in his preparation to teach deaf-mutes how to speak, he would not have been prepared to carry through this laborious task of inventing the telephone.

After a long, useful life, Alexander Graham Bell died on Wednesday morning, August 2, 1922, at his summer home near Baddeck, Cape Breton, Nova Scotia, "and was buried on the summit of Beinn Bhreagh in a grave blasted out of solid rock, overlooking the Bras d'Or Lakes and the surrounding country. During the simple ceremony on the mountain top, the entire telephone system of the United States and Canada, for a space of one minute, suspended service. No voice was heard upon the wires. There was silence over all telephone communication in tribute to him who had made telephone communication possible.

CHAPTER XIV

THE BOY WHO DID THINGS DIFFERENTLY.

JOHN, I shall be needing a helper today. A boy about your size will be quite strong enough to turn the bricks for me, I think."

Thus a tall, good-natured man addressed his small son one morning while putting on his coat and hat to go away to his work. And because John liked to be with his father, he cheerfully consented to be the helper needed for that day. So snatching his cap and flinging a kiss to his mother, he ran gaily down the path between the nodding hollyhocks and smiling marigolds to accompany his father to the brickyard.

John's father, Nelson Wanamaker, was a brickmaker. He owned a brickyard not far from the humble cottage that sheltered his happy family, in the southern outskirts of Philadelphia. Here he worked hard day after day to earn a living for his wife and growing family of boys and girls. John, the eldest, was born July 11, 1838; after him had come first a brother, William; then two sisters, Elizabeth, called by her father "Silver Heels," and Mary Ellen; two more brothers, Samuel and Francis Marion; and finally a baby sister, Bell.

On the edge of the Wanamaker brickyard stood a small frame schoolhouse where an old-fashioned schoolmaster taught the neighborhood children. Here John began his education as all boys do, learning how to read, write, and cipher. Every morning his mother waved good-by to him as he ran down the flower-bordered walk to the gate, and sometimes in the evening she came down the road to meet him as he returned from school. One wintry evening during his first term of school, John came home carrying a sheet of paper with embossed edges on which he had traced with ink the words the schoolmaster had written with lead pencil. He proudly approached his mother and gave the paper to her, and there she read the trembling tracing of these words:

"Peace on earth, good will to men!"[15] Although he had not yet learned how to read and write, John understood that the words he had traced so carefully conveyed a Christmas message. And to his sweet, gentle mother he presented the childish gift.

A few years later John entered another school near home and continued his studies there. He was often mentioned at school or at play as the boy "who wants to know more about things." Instead of being kept in by the teacher, he would sometimes keep the teacher in to explain difficult examples until he understood them. One of the books he prized highly from those boyhood days was an arithmetic bound in paper boards, which his mother had covered with pieces of cloth from a familiar worn-out dress. The sight of that closed book reminded him of how his mother used to look when she wore the dress, and so the arithmetic became a memory book, too.

As a schoolboy John seldom engaged in the rougher sports of his playmates. If he played ball he usually got hurt; if he went out to skate he was sure to fall down. And so he used to wander down the shady winding lanes alone and climb on the rail fence to sit and listen to the songs of the birds, or else sit down in a quiet corner to read. One of the books which

---

[15] Luke 2:14

used to hold his attention for hours at a time was the dictionary.

He would make collections of unfamiliar words and learn their meaning and how to use them correctly. Another book which interested him greatly was *Robinson Crusoe*. Again and again he read it through, and he always pictured in his imagination the lively activities and exciting experiences of the hero of the story.

Still another book that John treasured was *Pilgrim's Progress*. This book also set his imagination to work, and he followed the hero, Christian, with wide-awake interest through his thrilling adventures. But the book which in later life became to John the Book of books was the Bible. Just a boy he was when he first began to read from its pages, and never did he lose interest in reading the Bible until death closed his eyes at the advanced age of eighty-five. How many times he had read the good Book through we do not know, but with every reading he loved it better than before.

One afternoon when John, then a barefoot ten-year-old lad, was playing in a vacant lot near home, a stranger came by and stopped to speak to him. "We are going to begin a Sunday school in the Landreth schoolhouse," he said, "and we would like to have you and your brothers and sisters attend the school." A

Sunday school! John wondered what kind of a school that would be. So he went to find out the very first Sunday, and he liked the school so well that he continued to attend Sunday school regularly for the next seventy-five years. Finally, when he became an old man, he was elected president of the International Sunday School Association, which is interested in the Sunday schools all around the world. He himself then taught a class in Philadelphia whose membership ran well above one thousand. Sometimes there were more than two thousand in his class Sunday after Sunday.

One Sunday when John was eleven years old, the teacher of his class showed him a little red leather-bound Bible about eight inches long and six inches wide. "I should like to own such a Bible," said John, after he had examined it carefully.

"Then you may take this one home with you and pay for it as you earn the money," replied his teacher. John was delighted with the offer until he learned the price of the book. To him the amount of two dollars and seventy-five cents was an amazing sum, and he feared that he might never be able to earn that much money. But the teacher felt willing to trust him, and after many weeks had passed, John presented the last of the hard-earned copper coins necessary to pay the price of the Bible.

"This was the biggest purchase I ever made," said John when he became an old, old man. "Although I have bought property costing millions of dollars since then, I know the purchase of that little gilt-edged Bible meant more to me than any other purchase in my lifetime."

As John grew from boyhood, his father wished to have him learn the brickmaking trade. But John believed that he could prepare himself to do greater work. So at the age of fourteen he began work as an errand boy in a bookstore, earning one dollar and a quarter a week. He had to walk several miles from his home to his place of employment in the city, and until he reached the pavement, his way led through narrow lanes and across open fields and truck patches. In springtime and in autumn these country roads and lanes were often quite muddy, while during the summer they were covered with a thick layer of dust. In order to look as neat as possible when reaching his place of employment, John used to carry his shoes in his hands until he reached the pavement, thus keeping them clean from mud or dust.

One day John's father said, "Son, you can earn much more money as a brickmaker than you can by running errands."

"Yes," replied the boy, "but you see, I do not intend to run errands all my life. I expect some day to use my head instead of my legs to earn money. If I become a brickmaker, I will have to depend upon the use of my hands to make a living. I think I can make more out of myself by using my brain than you make by using your hands."

How John expected to use his brain Mr. Wanamaker did not know. He feared that the boy would not succeed, but like a wise father he let John try for himself. And so John continued to run errands for the bookstore. When he was sent on an errand he went straight to the place and returned as quickly as possible. The sight of an organ-grinder with a monkey could not draw his attention away from the world his employers expected him to remain focused on. Not even the clang of a fire bell could induce him to run out into the street and neglect his work. And while he worked, he kept his mind busy thinking and planning how he might improve himself and get ready to do great things in the future.

One day John heard that a stock boy was wanted in a clothing store near by, and that better wages would be paid than he was then receiving. So he quit working as an errand boy in the bookstore and found an opportunity in the clothing store to learn how to become a merchant. For several years he kept working for his new employer, and all the time he tried to make himself generally useful that he might learn more about the business. Although he worked for a small wage, he saved his money and planned to use it when he would go into business for himself.

One time a special lot of black neckties were given into his keeping. Although there were many of them, John had examined them so closely that when, in his absence at lunch time, his employer gave one to a friend, John missed it from the lot. Not knowing that his employer had taken the necktie, John set to work to trace its disappearance. So earnestly did he go after its recovery that finally he found out who had taken it. This carefulness on his part pleased his employer, who afterwards took quite an interest in John and helped him to learn more about the clothing business.

While still a young man, John Wanamaker decided to go into the clothing business himself. So he and a friend prepared to begin business in a tiny room which they had to fit up to become suitable for a store. Buying material with which to build shelves, counters, and other fixtures cost so much money that they had scarcely anything left with which to buy stock to sell.

"What shall we do?" asked his partner in despair.

"Get more stock," replied John, and off he went to see a wholesale merchant, telling him just what he wanted.

The merchant listened quietly, and when John had finished speaking he asked, "What can you give me for security?"

"The whole store and stock," John answered, showing him a carefully made list which included the value of everything, even to the shelves and counters.

Believing that John was an honest young man who would make good in business, the wholesale merchant let him select two hundred dollars' worth of stock, which was twice as much as John had intended to try to get.

John was not prepared to take the stock at once, and the merchant expected him to send a truck to deliver it to his store. Instead, John hurried away to borrow a wheelbarrow, and returned to haul it himself.

"Where is the truck?" asked the puzzled wholesaler.

Pointing to the wheelbarrow, John replied that he would do his own hauling.

"But you will have to make at least five trips," protested the wholesaler.

"I do not mind that," said John, setting to work to place the first load in the wheelbarrow. His willingness to work with his hands as well as to plan with his brain pleased the wholesaler, who felt that it would be safe to help this ambitious young man.

When John started out in business for himself, he decided to do things differently from other merchants. He began by advertising his business to draw the attention of people who might be wishing to make purchases. Always he advertised honestly, and always he treated his customers politely, making them feel at home in his store. If for any reason they were not pleased with their purchase, he agreed to refund their money to them and let them go elsewhere to buy. Other merchants at that time did not advertise; neither did they always treat their customers quite fair. John and his partner made many friends because of their honesty and courtesy, and their business grew and grew.

After his partner died, John built up a great business for himself. Not all at once, but year after year he added to his stock of goods until finally he had the greatest store in Philadelphia, with a floor space covering forty-five acres. In New York City he also purchased a wonderful store, which has become one of the show places of that marvelous city. And in both of these great stores he continued to add improvements for the accommodation of the people who came to do their shopping or merely to visit and see the sights. He was the first to provide the public comforts of free restrooms, toilets, telegraph and postal facilities, and package and checking-rooms without charge.

Not only did he treat his customers kindly, he also was careful to show kindness to the many clerks who stood behind the counters in his great stores and sold his stock. He provided schools for those who had been denied an education, and helped the young people in his employ who were trying to become successful businessmen and women.

As time passed by, John Wanamaker's friends realized that he had indeed found the way to use his brain and do great things. They saw that he was a very successful merchant, and more than that, a successful man. Whatever he undertook he did well, and he always worked to improved conditions for other people. For a while he served as Postmaster General, and we owe to him thanks for the rural delivery throughout our country.

During these busy years, John Wanamaker always took time to attend to his Christian duties. He was never too busy to help someone in trouble, and he found especial delight in talking to people about the heavenly Father. Every morning he read from the Bible and prayed with his family before going to the store, even when it meant that he would have to rise an hour earlier in order to catch the train to visit the store in New York. And when at last old age came on and he knew he could not live much longer, he said, "Dying is just like opening the door and going into my Father's house."

CHAPTER XV

The Boy Who Was Always Making Things.

ONE rainy afternoon in midsummer of 1863—July 30 it was—a baby boy was born into a comfortable farm house not far from Dearborn, Michigan. Just an ordinary baby boy, with an ordinary set of lungs, and an ordinary appetite, demanding the ordinary attention that all babies do—so he seemed to the neighbors and friends and relatives. But to his proud parents he seemed to be a most wonderful child, for he was their firstborn.

After due consideration the parents decided that he should become the namesake of his uncle, Henry Ford, who, with the baby's father, William Ford, had come from Ireland to America in 1847. So that name and the date of his birth was penned very carefully in the family record. And thus began the historical record of one of America's citizens whose fame now encircles the globe.

Henry's earliest memory carries him back to the large room in the farmhouse which served as kitchen, dining-room, and sitting-room. Here he used to follow his mother about and ask questions from morning until night. He wanted to know why the tops of the kettles and the pots jumped and danced under the pressure of the steam. He wanted to stand over the stove and watch the kettle of water boil and the white cloud pour out from the kettle spout. He wanted to know what would happen if that spout were shut tight enough to keep the steam from escaping. He was not satisfied with an explanation, but was always begging his mother to let him investigate everything for himself.

When Henry was six years old, his curiosity had grown so much that he felt the need of doing some experimenting. If only his mother would allow him to use the pots and kettles in the kitchen! But he knew she would not, so he set about to find a substitute. Presently he espied a thick, brown earthenware jug, which he believed would answer the purpose fairly well. So he filled it with water, stuffed the neck tightly with paper, and fastened it securely. Then he set it over the fire and waited to see what would happen next. What a dangerous thing for anyone to do! Before long the water came to a boil and then the jug exploded with a bang that shook the whole house. Coals of fire, boiling water, and pieces of jug were scattered all over the room. Even the window panes were broken, and the wonder is that Henry was not killed. As it was, he had his face badly burned with hot water and his head cut by a bit of the broken jug.

Now Henry understood why the kettle lids jumped and danced when the steam came pouring out from beneath. He understood that steam is something powerful, not to be bottled up tight, and never again did he attempt to do such a foolish thing. But when he grew to manhood he learned how to use steam power to help in his manufacturing.

Because Henry's father was a regular farmer, he often had scraps of wood and metal lying about the place. And because Henry was a regular boy, he used to collect these scraps and play with them. Sometimes he would find an old wheel from a worn-out machine, or an old spring, rusted bolts, knife blades, and such odds and ends. With these scraps he would make articles which he used as tools in his play.

But as Henry grew older, his playtime grew

less, for there were many little odd jobs on the farm that a small boy could do. He and his younger brother John were expected to keep the woodbox filled, to gather cobs from the pigpen, hunt the eggs, and bring kindling to start the morning fire. During harvest time they were sent several times a day with a cool, dripping jug of fresh water to the men at work in the fields. In the evening they brought up the cows from a shady pasture, they carried the milk pails to the barn, they filled the horses' mangers with hay, and they fed mush and milk to the young calves. There were ever so many things to be done about the farm, just as there always have been and always will be ever so many things for boys to do who grow up on the farm.

Not far from the Ford home, in opposite directions, were two little red schoolhouses. One of them was called the Scotch Settlement School, and the other was called the Miller School. Because the Ford farm was in the middle of the district, sometimes the children attended one school and sometimes the other.

Henry did not enter school until he was eight years old. Very likely his brother John accompanied him from the first day on. Henry already knew how to read and write, for a boy of his inquiring mind would naturally ask his mother to spell out the letters on the oven door, and on the oatmeal box, and on everything he saw from the time he was old enough to know about letters. And thus he may have learned how to read. Learning how to write may have begun by first tracing the letters in their printed form with a piece of chalk or with a pencil, and afterwards tracing them in their written form, just the simple process that everyone follows who first learns to read and write.

Henry's first teacher was a good man who took an interest in his pupils. Thus school life began smoothly for the Ford brothers, and Henry added daily to his stock of learning from schoolbooks. He studied his lessons and did his school work well. He also got along with his teachers, for he was a quiet, likable boy. Although pupils were frequently punished in the schools by whipping, Henry never had to undergo such a punishment.

Not that school life did not offer more to the boys than lessons and recitations, for there were recess periods and lively games out on the playground. Hi-spy, prisoner's base, fox and geese, dog and deer, leap-frog, pop the whip, and "Tom, Tom, pull away," were games they often played. Because hard rubber balls were scarce in the town near by, and money for playthings was even less plentiful, the boys manufactured a rubber ball for their sport. They nailed together three heels of worn-out rubber boots and cut them carefully into a round ball. This they used in all their games where a ball was needed. Of course the boys played marbles and "mumblety-peg," and they "skinned the cat."

But Henry was not satisfied always to play the same game over and over. He liked to make things, and even on the schoolground he used to put together odds and ends into useful articles. One time he suggested to the other boys that they build a dam across the creek that flowed near the schoolhouse. He would make a wooden water-wheel to fit in the race,[16] and the water flowing through would furnish the power to turn the wheel. So the boys set to work energetically and dammed the creek; then they made a race, and Henry brought his wheel to put into it.

But while this fun was going on, trouble was brewing up the creek. The water was overflowing in a farmer's potato field, and the farmer was doing some investigating. When he found out who was causing the damage to his potato crop, he complained to the schoolmaster, and that ended the fun. The boys learned from that experience that developing water power has other problems besides furnishing machinery and building water-tight dams.

One day, when Henry was twelve years old, a great sorrow came into his home, for his mother died. What a true friend she had always been to her children! And how sadly

---

[16] A canal for a current of water.

they missed her! Never again did home seem quite the same to Henry after that, for no one could fill the empty place she used to fill so well. "The house was like a watch without a mainspring," said Henry after his mother had died.

But the farm work continued to go on the same rounds as before. The boys were wakened each morning at daylight in summer and before daylight in winter to help do the morning chores. There were cows to be milked, the stock to be fed, and water to be pumped every morning the year round before the call to breakfast. Everybody worked, and Henry did his share. By the time he was twelve years old, he could follow the plow down the long furrows in the field and do almost a man's work.

Henry did not like to work on a farm. He did not like to milk cows or care for horses. However, he did not slight his work, and his father believed that some day he would become a real farmer, for whatever Henry had to do, he did well whether he liked to do it or not. One thing which did greatly interest him on the farm was the machinery. He learned how to operate every new piece of machinery that his father bought. And he studied each machine so carefully that soon he knew how to take it to pieces and put it together again. He learned how to repair broken machinery and tools, and when the neighbors found out what he could do, they brought their repair work to him also. This kind of work he did at odd times, and nowhere about the farm was he so satisfied as when working in the shop.

One day when Henry was nearly thirteen years old, he went with his father to town. As they were jogging slowly along the road in a wagon, they met a road engine which had a chain connecting it with the rear wheels of the vehicle on which it was mounted. This was the first "motor car" that Henry had ever seen. The engineer, not wishing to frighten the horses which Mr. Ford was driving, stopped the engine beside the road to allow them to pass. This was Henry's opportunity. With a bound he sprang from the wagon to the ground and ran over to look at that strange new engine. He climbed onto its platform and asked the driver all about how the engine was operated. And not until he had looked the engine over most carefully and asked all kinds of questions about it did he dismount and return to the wagon.

From that day Henry began to think about building an engine. The first one that he made was built of wood. For the boiler he used a five-gallon oil can. Next he built one from metal scraps, and this one really ran. Still he wanted to know more about mechanics, so he began to read books and magazines that helped to explain how things are made. He would try out these new ideas and learn as much in the tool shop as he did from the books and magazines.

At first Henry's father did not mind when the boy spent so much time with machinery. He thought it was a fine thing for a farmer to know how to mend his own implements, and he felt proud of Henry's skill. But as the boy grew older and continued to grow more interested in making things, his father began to worry. Suppose Henry would not want to become a farmer, after all! And sure enough, when Henry finished his school work in the neighborhood, he came one day to tell his father that he wanted to go to Detroit and find work in a machine-shop.

"You will be making a great mistake to leave the farm," reasoned his father.

But when Henry assured him that he felt no interest in farming and that he wanted very much to learn how to build machines, his father finally consented to let him go and seek new opportunities in the city.

At the first machine-shop where he applied for work, the foreman was in need of extra helpers, so Henry found a place at once. "Come tomorrow morning," the foreman said, "and I will put you on at two dollars and fifty cents a week."

"I'll be right here," answered Henry, and off he went to find a place to sleep.

But finding a place to sleep was quite a problem. Cheap beds were not clean like the beds back on the farm, and a decent bed would cost more than he could afford to pay when he had to buy three meals a day besides. He saw at once that he would have to earn more money if he wished to live decently. So after supper he applied for work in a watchmaker's shop, where the owner worked at night to repair watches. Back at home Henry had quite a reputation in the neighborhood as a clock and watch repairer, so he believed he could do this kind of work. The man agreed to pay him two dollars a week for working four hours each night, beginning at seven o'clock. This amount would be enough, added to his day's wages, to pay all his expenses. So Henry went to work with a happy heart.

For nine months he worked from seven o'clock in the morning until six o'clock in the evening in the machine shop, then from seven until eleven in the watchmaker's shop, for a while earning only four dollars and fifty cents a week. His father came to visit him and urged him to return to the farm where he would not have to work such long hours, but Henry liked the shop work better than farming. He was learning how to use new tools and how to make things in real earnest. What more did he need to make him happy?

When Henry entered young manhood, he returned to help his father with the farm work one winter and, much to his father's delight, he decided to try farming for himself. All went well for a while, but the time came again when he felt that he had other work to do in the world besides raising crops and livestock. He felt that he must make something to lighten the labor of farmers; so again he returned to Detroit and went to work, this time for the Edison Electric Company. Here he lived in the hum of machinery, learning more about it all the time and also learning about electricity.

The dream of Henry's life had been to make a machine that would take the place of horses on the farm. At first he had no intentions of making a car in which to ride, but rather a machine to use for plowing and for doing all kinds of farm work. But when he saw that farmers would accept a touring car quicker than a substitute for horses in the field, he set to work to build such a car for them. For a long while he spent all of his spare time in a little shop at the rear of his home in Detroit trying to build such a car. Everybody laughed at his idea except his wife. She believed that he would succeed.

One rainy morning, Henry Ford rushed into the house to tell his wife that the car on which he had worked so long would now run and that he was going to give it a trial out in the street. So she took an umbrella and ran out-of-doors in the rain to see her husband start his horseless carriage and ride away. Sure enough, it was a success! It would run, and run fast.

But Henry Ford's hard work was not ended yet. He had made a car that would run; now he needed to make a car that people would want to drive. So he continued to add improvements until he had built an attractive little car which people admired. Then he was ready to place his car on the market.

Twenty-five years later, horseless carriages left a trail of dust behind them on every crossroad, down every highway, and glided with certainty over every accessible mountain pass in the world. And most prominent among them were the practical little machines called "Fords," which were close of kin to the queer little four-wheeled horseless vehicle that Henry Ford first drove through the streets of Detroit. He had manufactured a car which filled the need of the working man who cannot afford to drive an expensive automobile. And because the working man represents the majority of the world's population, Henry Ford led the world in the manufacture of gasoline motor cars.

CHAPTER XVI

Two Brothers Who Did What Couldn't Be Done!

FOR long, long years people had been thinking, "Would it not be wonderful if we could soar in the air like birds?" But they had been saying, "If God intended for men to fly, he would have given them wings."

But every now and then someone happened along who wanted to learn how to fly. "We have minds capable of thinking and planning and discovering things unknown to us before," those persons said, "and we might be able to make wings with which to fly." So they would try, and try, and try again, and just as often they would fail to discover the secret of flying. Other people laughed at them for spending their time foolishly trying to do what couldn't be done! Finally someone wrote an amusing story about "Darius Green and His Flying Machine,"[17] and people who read the story supposed that only simple-minded persons called "half-wits" would try such ridiculous stunts as learning how to fly.

No one enjoys being laughed at, and everyone shrinks from being called a simpleton. Great courage is required on the part of anyone who will dare to follow his convictions when he knows that by doing so his neighbors and friends will think he is losing his mind. But now and then somebody who possesses the needed courage dares to try to do what he believes can be done, and after trying again and again he proves by and by that he is right. The world owes much to the bravery of such intelligent men who will keep right on studying and experimenting until they succeed in the inventions they have set out to make. Listed among such courageous men we find the names of Wilbur and Orville Wright, inventors of the airplane.

These two brothers were the sons of a minister, Bishop Milton Wright. Wilbur, the elder, was born near Millville, Indiana, on the sixteenth of April, 1867, and four years later, on the nineteenth of August, 1871, Orville was

---

[17] Poem written by John T. Trowbridge (1827-1916).

born in Dayton, Ohio.

The difference in age did not prevent these brothers from becoming playmates and sharing their toys together. Orville's chubby fingers were not denied the pleasure of clasping Wilbur's playthings and examining them to his heart's delight. Nor did he suffer the painful child-hurts known to some small brothers who are called "tag-along," and are sent weeping back to the house when the older boys start out on a hike.

Although Bishop Wright was a busy man, he took time to think about the needs of his growing children. He remembered how it felt to be a boy, and when he saw interesting toys in the shop windows he knew his sons would be delighted to play with them. Sometimes he would step inside the shop and ask the clerk to wrap up a certain toy which particularly attracted his attention and which he believed his boys would appreciate. Just one toy would be enough for the two boys; they played together.

One evening the bishop came home with a bulging package tucked beneath his arm. Wilbur, then aged eleven, and Orville, aged seven, were so occupied with their play that they did not see him unwrap the package. They scarcely heard him enter the room; but when he said, "Here's something for you, boys!" they glanced up to see a strange object dart through the air and bump against the ceiling, then fall to the floor.

"What is it?" they cried, as they ran to pick it up.

"Scientists call it a helicopter," explained their father.

"Let's call it a 'bat,'" suggested one of the boys, and to this the other one agreed. Their other game forgotten, now they gave full attention to the maneuvers of the "bat." Again and again they picked the crumpled toy from the carpet, twisted the rubber bands tightly, and hurled it through the air. And just as often they laughed to see it buzz about overhead, bump against the wall or the ceiling, and fall limply to the floor. What fun they did have with that "bat"! But presently the rubber bands snapped, and then the delicate, paper-covered wings could fly no more. The fun was over; the broken "bat" was tossed aside. But Wilbur and Orville Wright were unknowingly started on the road to fame.

One day when Orville had grown old enough to help make playthings, the boys decided to build another "bat" like the one their father had bought at the shop. So they made a light frame similar to the cork-and-bamboo frame of their broken toy and covered it with paper. Then they took two rubber bands and adjusted them so that when they were tightly twisted they would drive the paper-covered wings in opposite directions. When all was ready, they threw the homemade toy into the air and it flew just as the shop toy had flown. They had built their first flying-machine!

"We'll make a bigger one now," they decided, after watching the first one fly about. But they learned that a bigger "bat" could not fly so well as a smaller sized one. "Something is wrong," they agreed; "but what is it?" Neither of them could find out; so finally they grew tired of making small "bats" and decided to manufacture kites instead.

Building kites seemed better sport than building "bats," for kites can fly high above the treetops and do not bump into the sky. Sometimes the strings tangle in the telegraph wire and sometimes they break and let the kite fly away. But on the whole Wilbur and Orville had much fun playing with their kites. While watching them glide upward and soar about overhead, the boys used to think how much fun it would be to make a kite big enough to carry a man in it.

The Wright brothers did not spend all their time at play. They attended school in Dayton and took an interest in their studies, for they found out that schoolbooks answer some of the questions of why and how that they had often asked each other. And as they grew older they began to read other books and magazines.

Orville decided that he would like to enter the printing business. So when he was still a lad, he built a printing press with odd bits of wood and string and secured some type. Then he began to print a boy's paper called *The Midget*. He succeeded so well that finally he bought a better outfit and began to print a weekly newspaper called *The West Side News*. Wilbur became editor of the paper and Orville remained the publisher; thus the two brothers worked together as they had played together when they were children.

Just as kite-flying had once afforded them out-of-door sport, now bicycle-riding became their favorite hobby. They became expert riders on their bicycles and entered races with other contestants. They took pride in keeping their wheels in good condition and did their own repair work. After a while they grew more interested in bicycles than in the printing business, so they opened a shop where they built and repaired bicycles. While engaged in this business, they studied mechanics very carefully and learned how to make improvements on their bicycles. Every bit of work that passed through their hands was well done, for they were painstaking workmen. Building bicycles was just as much fun to them as building "bats" had been when they were boys. And always their customers were well pleased with the work done in Wright Brothers' repair shop.

The years passed by and Wilbur and Orville grew to manhood, working together just as happily as they had played together. One day in autumn of 1896, they read in the newspaper an account of the death of a German inventor who had been trying to learn how to fly. This man had built wing-like devices called "gliders," and with these he had made more than two thousand glides through the air. Then while experimenting in this manner, he had lost this life.

The Wright brothers had never forgotten their boyhood interest in building flying toys. They remembered how they used to build kites stronger and better than any of their friends could build. They knew that their love for flying kites had been so strong they might have continued the sport all the way through the years had they not grown too big to mingle with the kite-flying boys of the town. And so they had been compelled to put away their flying apparatus and take up other interests more becoming to young men.

Now as they worked together in their bicycle shop they talked the matter over and decided to take up kite manufacturing again.

"People will laugh at us and call us fools," they said; "but we will let them laugh. This time we will build a kite strong enough to carry a passenger."

So they set to work to build something like a box-kite, having two parallel planes that they held by a light line. Then they tried to fly this machine in a strong wind. Each of them made daring experiments while trying to ride the great kite, but finally they admitted failure. Their machine needed more power than the wind supplied to lift it from the earth with a passenger in it.

Now the brothers realized that they needed to understand more about the air and about engineering. Neither of them had attended college, but both of them set to work to study and learn all that could be learned from books and magazines. As they studied, they experimented to find out whether the book-knowledge was workable. Whenever they found it was at fault, they kept on experimenting until they learned the right thing to do. For several years they studied and worked until finally they had no more money with which to experiment.

The people who used to have business dealings with the Wright brothers shook their heads and said it was a pity that those fine young fellows had lost their heads over trying to make a silly invention. They did not believe people would care to risk their lives flying even if someone should discover how the trick could be done.

But there was one person living in Dayton who believed Wilbur and Orville Wright were on the track of a great invention. That person was their sister, Katherine. Now she was teaching school and earning a small salary, a part of which she willingly lent to help her brothers when their money was exhausted. With this money they were able to go on with their work until finally they invented the airplane.

Wilbur went to France in 1908 and there he successfully demonstrated his ability to control his plane while in the air. Because of this achievement, he won great public honors, including the Michelin Prize. The following year he gave public demonstrations before the King of Spain, the King of England, and the King of Italy, convincing them that he had mastered the long-sought art of flying. At home Orville was giving public performances with his plane, and soon the Wright brothers found themselves the most talked of men in the world. Now medals, degrees, titles, and money came to them in reward for their faithful, persistent effort to prove to mankind the possibility of making a successful flying-machine.

In the hour of triumph, these brothers did not forget that they owed their sister a share of their honors, for she had been the one who helped them scramble across the threshold to fame. She had encouraged them to go on when others laughed at them. And when they had needed money to complete their experiments she had supplied their lack. Now when honors were heaped upon them they insisted that she share a part.

After they had succeeded in building machines that could fly, Wilbur and Orville worked just as hard trying to improve them as they had worked in their bicycle shop when they used to make improvements on their wheels. They continued to work together and to study the problems of flight until May 30, 1912, when Wilbur died of typhoid fever. Then Orville pursued his studies alone, and later on he became chief engineer of the Wright Aeronautical Company and director of its laboratory at Dayton, Ohio.

Because of the patience, determination, and skill of these brothers, the world now possesses the most rapid means of transportation known in the history of man. Where formerly days, weeks, and months were required to cross continents and oceans, now these distances can be spanned by planes in hours by the clock. Less than twenty-five years after the first plane lifted itself into the air, brave young adventurers such as Colonel Charles Lindbergh made non-stop flights across the Atlantic from America to France, while Commander Richard E. Byrd took his plane over the dangerous ice of the North Pole. By that time airplanes were being used to carry passengers and mail across the country, to aid in mapmaking, in forest protection, in exploration, and in advertising. And every plane that flies in any part of the world carries the same means of control which were first invented by Wilbur and Orville Wright.

CHAPTER XVII

The Boy Who Learned How To Use What Others Wasted.

ONE bright spring morning a nine-year-old lad saw a turkey hen steal away into the woods near his country home.

"She is going out there to lay her eggs and hatch her baby turkeys," reasoned the lad. "And I know that half of those little turkeys will never live to grow up if they are left alone in the woods. I will find her next and watch until the eggs hatch; then I'll bring the little chicks home and care for them right."

With this determination young John set out to find the hidden nest, and for days he searched the wood lot before he located its whereabouts.

Then he watched patiently until the eggs were hatched and the young chicks were ready to remove from their wild surroundings to the barnyard premises. From this moment his real task began.

"Mother, see what I've found!" he exclaimed as he proudly presented the turkey family at the kitchen door. "These are the chicks that hatched from those eggs in the nest I found out in the woods."

Like all good mothers, Mrs. Rockefeller paused in her busy hour to take time to look at John's finding and to praise him for his success in capturing the young chicks before they darted away out of reach in the thick underbrush.

"If you will take care of them now that you have brought them from their hiding-place in the woods," said his mother, "I will give them to you."

"For my very own?" asked John, happily.

"Yes, for your very own," replied his mother with a smile.

So John hurried away to establish safely his turkey family in an empty coop for their new home, and immediately he began plans to raise them carefully.

"They must have plenty to eat," he reasoned; "and then they will grow."

"I s'pose they'll need water, too, like Mother's

other chicks," he added as an afterthought. So away he ran to find an empty can and a clean board to use for a feeding trough.

And a busy lad John was all through the following summer, for never once did he forget to ask his mother for scraps from the kitchen and for curds from the milk to feed his growing turkeys. "If I feed them well they will grow fast," he told himself again and again. "And when they are grown I shall take them to town and sell them."

John was not long in discovering that there is more work connected with raising turkeys than simply feeding them plenty to eat and keeping plenty of drinking water in their vessels. For, being turkeys, they insisted on running about to chase bugs, and sometimes they wandered far from their home near the barnyard. Sometimes they were caught in out-of-the-way places when a sudden summer shower came pouring down, and then John had the task of searching for them and bringing them, drenched and shivering, into the kitchen to dry.

Finally, after the weeks passed by into months, John's turkeys grew as large as the mother hen and were ready for sale. So they were again caught, one by one, and this time they were carried away to market. When John returned home that day, he proudly deposited his first hard-earned money in a china dish on the mantel—he had made his start toward becoming a self-supporting citizen of the United States of America.

More than seventy years after John sold his turkeys at the market in Moravia, New York, he returned one summer day to revisit the scenes of his childhood. Up and down the green-clad hills he motored until he came to the old, old house on Michigan Hill, four miles from Richford, where on July 9, 1839, he had been born. Not far distant were the peaceful waters of Owasco Lake where he had learned how to swim and how to catch fish. How well he recalled those happy days of long ago!

In the Rockefeller home there had been a younger brother, William, a sister, Mary, and then the twins—Franklin and Frances. There had been plenty of chores to do about the home, and John was a willing helper. He knew the thrills of following his father into the forests where the great trees fell beneath the axmen's strokes. He followed on to the sawmill which his father had built, and there he saw the trees made into lumber. He buried his bare toes into the sawdust; he gathered chips for kindling; he carried wood for the kitchen fire. And by and by he grew responsible enough to feed and milk the cow every morning and evening. Then, too, there was the home garden to be weeded during the growing months, and John shared his part of this task also. What a busy lad he was during those years spent on the farm!

Schooldays shared a part in John's early life, and when he reached the age of fourteen he was ready to enter high school. At that time his parents had moved to Cleveland, Ohio, where there were better educational advantages than could be offered on the farm. Here John manifested an especial interest in mathematics and music, and learned to play on the piano. Because he was studious he made good progress during the two years that he attended the Cleveland high school. Then he attended the Commercial College and prepared himself to enter the business world.

Soon after coming to Cleveland, John began to attend church services regularly. He felt interested in the preaching services and in the mid-week prayer-meetings, as well as in the Sunday school. "I must find some way to become a useful member in this church," he said, and so he looked about to see what he might do. Every little opportunity for service he was glad to improve, for he believed that every little bit of good accomplished helped just that much. When he had lived in Cleveland about one year he decided to help pay off the church debt. This seemed a huge undertaking

for a lad of fifteen years earning no salary, but
John dared to try to do it. He gave of his own
money all that he could; then he set about to
urge others to follow his example. Standing
in the church-door as the people passed, he
invited them one by one to help pay off the debt.
Because of his interest in the church affairs he
was made one of the board of trustees before
he reached the age of twenty.

When John finished his course in the
Commercial College he set out to find work.
Day after day he walked the streets, visiting
manufacturing establishments, stores, and
shops, again and again, but everywhere he
went he found nothing to do. A less courageous
young man would have become discouraged
and quit, but John was determined to find what
he was looking for. After a six weeks' search
he found employment as assistant bookkeeper
in a commission house, where he went to work
in earnest, not knowing what his salary would
be. For three months he worked and then came
his first pay envelope. In it he found fifty dollars, which averaged less than four dollars a
week. But John was satisfied with this small
amount for a beginning, and kept steadily at
work. The next year his salary was increased
to twenty-five dollars a month, and by the
third year he was promoted to the position of
cashier and bookkeeper, with a salary of five

hundred dollars a year.

From early childhood John had been taught by his parents to believe that work is honorable, and that neither time nor money should be spent foolishly. Now that he was entering young manhood, he wished to start a business for himself. He talked the matter over with his friend, Morris Clark, and they decided to form a partnership and establish a produce commission firm. In order to do this John would need two thousand dollars, and his saving at the bank amounted to only one-half of the needed sum. His father, believing that John would make a prosperous businessman, lent him the other one thousand dollars at ten percent interest, and soon afterwards the firm of Clark and Rockefeller was doing a good business. More than a year passed by when one day, Mr. Rockefeller called John and said, "Son, you have made a good beginning in your business venture, and I see that you are keeping the interest paid up on the money I lent you. Now you have reached your twenty-first birthday, and I shall give that money to you for a present."

Not far from his home city in the neighboring state of Pennsylvania, the first oil-well had been drilled in America less than a year before that time. John and his partner had read a great deal in the newspapers about the excitement produced among the people by that marvelous well, and they felt a curiosity to see it. They had heard that springs of petroleum had been discovered in Ohio long before, and that the oil had been used in lamps in workshops. But nothing had been done to develop the oil industry, although far-sighted men had predicted that the day would come when oil would be used for lighting the street-lamps.

One day John decided to visit the oilfield and look the business over thoroughly. "If it proves to be a paying investment," he and his partner reasoned, "we may do well to establish an oil-refining business in Cleveland." The trip to Titusville, on Oil Creek, a branch of the Allegheny River, had its thrills for John, for he found the oilfield located in a rough country where the roads were almost impassible. On the first day out he had a never-to-be-forgotten experience. While investigating the nature of the work, John and his companion had to cross a ravine on a rotten plank.

"Do you think we can make it?" asked John's companion.

Looking thoughtfully upon the slimy, oil-surfaced depths of slush beneath the plank, John replied, "Is there no way around?"

"I fear not," came the answer.

"Then," said John, "there is nothing like trying."

First his companion crossed, but John slipped, falling with such a great splash into the ravine. Covered with oil from head to foot, he scrambled to the opposite bank.

"I see," said his companion humorously, "that you have plunged into this oil business head over heels."

"Judging from my appearance, I undoubtedly have," replied John, with a grin, looking down on the ruins of his best suit of clothes.

But he had come to investigate the oil industry, and he could not allow himself to be turned aside from his purpose by such an unfortunate accident; so John proceeded on his way until he had examined the work to his entire satisfaction. On his return home he was influential in establishing an oil refinery under the firm name of Andrews, Clark and Company. The business increased so rapidly that he sold his interest in the commission house and invested more money in oil.

Although John worked early and late, he always took time for his religious duties. Instead of going about with gay companions to places of idle amusement, he liked to visit sick people and cheer them with his friendly smile and quiet conversation. He found pleasure in trying to bring comfort to folks who were in trouble and distress. Also he improved his opportunities to invite strangers to the weekly prayer-meetings and to bring new pupils to Sunday school. Because of his friendly, big-brotherly interest in the boys and girls, he was chosen to be superintendent of the Sunday school, and for many years he served in that office. How the children loved him!

John gave the same whole-hearted attention to his business interests that he gave to his religious duties. And because he possessed good judgment, planning his undertakings carefully and wisely, he became a financial leader while yet a young man. He saw in the oil industry opportunities to develop great things, and at once he set about to make the most of those opportunities. Just as he recovered the young turkeys, which otherwise would have died of neglect, and nursed them into a paying profit when he was a small boy, now he took notice of things which other people overlooked and developed them into worthwhile products to place on the world market. Soon the name of John D. Rockefeller was known wherever the oil industry was introduced, for he became president of the Standard Oil Company. Again and again he was referred to as the wealthiest man in the world, but for all his wealth he continued to be a quiet, pleasant-faced, industrious man.

The time came when John retired from active business and devoted his energies to the huge task of giving away his millions. Not carelessly, but thoughtfully, he studied the needs of the human family in order to present his gifts where they would do the most good.

Through his lavish gifts colleges and universities have been founded, rural education among the neglected poor has been encouraged, and farming methods in the South have been improved. Also diseases have been studied. With the means supplied by the Rockefeller Institute for Medical Research, great discoveries such as the cause of the yellow fever plague have been made, and the terror of this and of other perils has been largely removed. Quietly and modestly this honorable man has given away his millions, preferring not to call attention to himself, but rather to benefit his fellowman.

CHAPTER XVIII

THE BOY WHO LOVED MUSIC.

IN the garden-spot of Russia—Podolia— there once lived a gentleman farmer and his wife whom the outside world came to hear about through their illustrious son, Ignace Jan Paderewski. This son was born to them on November 6, 1860. Little did they realize when they penned his name on the family register that some day the world would do him honor because of his remarkable skill as a musician.

A blue-eyed, golden-haired child, little Ignace brought joy to the hearts of his devoted parents. Like all babies of all generations he cooed and cried, he ate and slept, he grew and grew until he became quite strong enough to scramble out of the cradle unaided and toddle about the house. Then with the usual inquisitiveness of babyhood, he began to "get into things." Time and again, to keep him out of mischief, his mother took him onto her lap while she sat at the piano playing. And there, wide-eyed with wonder and delight, he watched her fingers glide smoothly and nimbly over the keys. Nor was the watching of those dear fingers the only charm which held him spellbound on his mother's lap—he thrilled at the sound of the musical tones which came from the instrument.

When baby Ignace grew old enough to appreciate his surroundings more fully, he discovered that he had a little sister to share with him the love of his devoted mother. What happy hours these children spent together, amusing themselves with their simple toys! And so the days, weeks, and months passed in that quiet country home, and baby Ignace grew into a fine little boy.

One day a great sorrow entered the home of the Paderewskis, for the mother took very, very ill. No more could the children feel the affectionate pressure of her gentle hand or see the lovelight shine from her smiling eyes, for she died. Soon another sorrow followed. Some cruel Russian soldiers came to the country homestead, seized the father roughly, clasped fetters of iron upon his wrists, and dragged him away to a cold, bleak country called Siberia. There they compelled him to work like a slave. Because they had suspected him of being unfriendly toward the Russian government, these soldiers had treated him so roughly and had banished him from his home and children to a land of strangers and of hardship.

Now little three-year-old Ignace and his sister were left like orphans. Kind people cared for them, giving them a home with plenty of food to eat; nice, warm clothes to wear; and a clean, soft bed in which to sleep. But there was no dear mother to call them in from play at lunchtime, to kiss away the hurt from their bumps and bruises, to listen to them lisp their evening prayers and tuck them snugly into bed. There was no kind father near to try to comfort them when they felt unhappy and to praise them when they did their best.

In spite of these sorrows little Ignace continued to grow straight and taller every year; and after several years had passed by, one glad day the news came that his father was returning from the land of exile, a freed man. How eagerly the children watched at the gate for his arrival! And how delightedly they flung themselves into his open arms when finally he came!

Through tears of joy Mr. Paderewski looked

into the upturned faces of his son and daughter and realized that they were safe and well. He saw, too, that during his absence they had been growing farther and farther away from babyhood, and that now they should be getting acquainted with schoolbooks. "My children must have a good education," thought he, so he began to plan at once how he might engage the best teachers for them. One day he saw Ignace sitting at the piano his mother had loved to play, and drumming upon the keys. Just a simple little melody of his own composition he was playing, but his father was pleased. "I shall do my utmost," he resolved, "to give the lad a musical education." So he made arrangements with an old teacher to visit the homestead once a month and instruct his children how to play the piano.

So few and far between were those early music lessons that Ignace could not advance rapidly in the beginning of his study of music. He found plenty of time to practice each lesson well before the teacher came to hear him recite. And he also found time to compose little melodies for his own entertainment. While his friends were dreaming about the time when they would grow up and become rich and powerful rulers in the land, he was thinking about the beautiful music which he would some day write for other artists to play. "The world will hear of my music some day," he would tell himself, "and the world will be glad. I must study hard, practice well, and learn everything that I possibly can about music, so I can give the very best kind of music to the world when I write." With this determination he continued his studies at home until his twelfth year, when his father arranged for his future education in the city.

Warsaw, the capital of Poland, was the city where his father sent him to school. There he was able to have regular music lessons at the Warsaw Conservatory, with the best teachers of which his country could boast. However much the twelve-year-old lad missed the freedom and quiet of the country, he did not complain, for now he could pursue his one great ambition to his heart's delight. True, there were other subjects besides music to be mastered, for in order to become a great composer he would need to understand the longings and the needs of his fellowmen. So he studied other languages and learned from reading their books what the people of other nations think, and feel, and desire. He also studied mathematics, and the various subjects taught in schools of higher learning. But always he returned with the greatest enthusiasm to his study of music and to his practice at the piano.

After spending four years in school at

Warsaw, Ignace began to give public concerts. From one place to another he went throughout the country, playing his own compositions before the audiences to see whether they appreciated his writings. During his first tour he came to a certain small town where he had announced a concert and found that there was no piano in the hall where the concert would be given. Of course he could not play without a piano, so the search began. Was there anybody in the town whose instrument they might hire for the night? No, that was not the question. Was there anybody in the town who had a piano? Only one piano could be found in the whole town, and that one was so badly out of tune that the hammers refused to return to the keys after they had been struck. What should be done? The crowd was beginning to assemble in the audience room, and the youthful musician had to think quickly.

"Bring the old piano over," he ordered, "and we shall see what we can do."

While several men were bringing the piano, another hurried away to bring a whip, and then a strange experiment took place. Ignace struck the chords, and an attendant struck the stubborn hammers with the whip when they refused to come down. And, wonder of wonders, it worked! So the unusual concert began, and "Bang!" went the chords, and "Swish!"

went the whip, much to the amusement and entertainment of the entire audience.

Ignace was only sixteen. When he finished that tour he felt he should return to Warsaw and resume the study of music before attempting to give more concerts. So he enrolled again at the Conservatory as a student of the piano and continued his studies until he was eighteen. Then he was appointed professor of music at the Conservatory.

At first the appointment pleased him, for he was still very young and did not realize that teaching music might be tiresome work. But when day after day passed by, with pupils coming for instruction from morning to night, Ignace grew restless. He had little time to call his own and no time to continue his studies. Instead of enjoying his work he began to dread it. So at the end of the term he gave up the work of professorship in Warsaw and went to Germany.

In Berlin, Ignace studied composition with two capable teachers, for he still longed to compose music for others to play. Then he consented to accept another appointment as pianoforte teacher at the Strasburg Conservatory, where he remained for a few years. During this time he met a celebrated actress from his homeland who took an interest in his artist career. She urged him to continue his studies and prepare to give concerts, for she believed that he possessed rare talent as a musician. "The world will applaud you as a genius of the finest type," she said. Finally Ignace yielded to her persuasion and went to Vienna to study under a famous teacher for nearly four more years. He was already an accomplished musician, having taught music to advanced pupils for several years. But he realized that if he hoped to do his very best he must do better tomorrow than he did today. At the end of his first year in Vienna he appeared in concert, and was greatly applauded. But he refused to allow this degree of success already attained to become his greatest, for he continued to study longer.

Then, after having spent long, hard years of study and work, Ignace at last started out to let the world of music-lovers hear him play. First he went to Paris, where the French music-lovers received him questioningly, wondering if he could please. But when they heard him they were thrilled, and for the entire season they enjoyed his concerts.

Soon the English music-lovers in London heard about the famous young artist who had charmed Paris folk with his skill at the piano, and they began to wonder whether, after all, he was as wonderful as he had been advertised. Ignace Paderewski did not compel them to remain wondering long, for he went to London at his first opportunity. And the English music-lovers, like the French, found out that he was indeed deserving of their greatest praise.

By the time the new pianist had become famous in Europe, for both the French and the English people appreciated him greatly. Now he looked out across the broad Atlantic Ocean and thought of the music-lovers of America. They, too, must have an opportunity to hear him and judge for themselves whether or not he could please. So he bade his European friends good-by and sailed for New York.

Music-lovers in America were wondering, just as other music-lovers in France and in England, what kind of impression this Polish artist would make in their midst. They were wondering whether he deserved all the praise which Paris and London had given him. And they came to hear him for the first time, not at all sure that they would appreciate him as an artist. But they went away satisfied; they had been convinced that he belonged to them just as much as he belonged to the Old World, for he understood the longings of music-loving people everywhere.

On his first visit to America, Ignace Paderewski stayed six months and gave no less than one hundred and seventeen recitals. So greatly was he appreciated that he was urged to return the next season and play again for the American people. His second visit was even more successful than the first. Everywhere he went crowds gathered to hear him; special trains were run from neighboring cities to accommodate the people who could not otherwise attend the concerts. In Texas, whole schools marched many miles to hear him, and such was the interest aroused by his personality that crowds frequently waited at railway stations merely to see the train pass, in hopes of catching a glimpse of his remarkable countenance. Sometimes crowds would line the streets from his hotel to the concert hall.

Because of the vastness of the American continent, visiting artists found tours through the country to be very exhausting. Going from city to city, and lodging in first one hotel, then another, is very unsatisfactory and wearing on the nerves of sensitive folk such as artists. Ignace Paderewski preferred to travel in a private car, having his own regular cook, who prepared his meals at the hours he wished to eat. In the observation room of the car where he made himself at home was a piano, for he still felt the need to practice in order to do his best. When preparing for a recital tour, he seldom practiced less than ten or twelve hours a day, and then he would often lie awake at night thinking about each part of the program.

Although Ignace Paderewski's greatest

youthful ambition was not to become a famous pianist, but rather to compose musical numbers for famous artists to play, nevertheless he found himself listed among the most famous pianists the world has known. He loved music and, loving it, he came to feel that music was a very part of himself. Then, in his effort to share with others the beauty he found in music, he gave himself in hard toil and study. Now, wherever his name is spoken, it is associated with the thought of musical art.

Do you see a man diligent in his work?
He will stand before kings.
                                        Proverbs 22:29

THE END.

ADDENDUM

A few days after reading about the life of John Wanamaker, I learned that his forty-five acre Philadelphia department store is the present-day *Lord and Taylor* department store. You cannot walk into this store without being in awe of its beauty. From the floor to the ceiling of the second-story mezzanine, you feel as though you have just stepped into a cathedral. In fact, the Wanamaker building hosts the largest pipe organ in the world—the Wanamaker. Imagine seeing the world's largest pipe organ in a department store!

John Wanamaker was building much more than a department store—he was building an appreciation for excellence and a monument that would reflect the beauty of his God and Savior. John Wanamaker introduced a paradigm shift and actually created a cultural revolution. Department stores were never quite the same after he set the standard.

Today, megastores such as Wal-Mart, Home Depot, and Sam's Club have created a paradigm shift and cultural change as well, but there is something significantly different when compared to the Wanamaker department store. One hundred years from now, the stores of today will most likely be non-existent, but the Wanamaker store will undoubtedly be admired for its beauty and history for many years to come.

John Wanamaker believed that if you were going to invest your time in something, then it was worth doing well. In fact, he believed that it ought to be done better than anyone else had done it before.

Today, the Wanamaker store, with the world's largest pipe organ, is a National Historic Landmark. To give you a sense of this grand masterpiece, when compared to the Notre Dame Cathedral in Paris, which features 8,000 pipes on its impressive organ, or the Mormon Tabernacle's pipe organ in Salt Lake City, which boasts 11,623 pipes, the Wanamaker dwarfs them all with 28,482 pipes. Not only is the organ a masterpiece, the pipes themselves are a wonder. Some are large enough for a child to crawl though, and the sugar-pine chambers that house them extend for seven stories! Since 1911, this organ resounds twice a day. Rather than listening to the latest "top twenty," shoppers listen to Mendelssohn or Mozart. People come from around the world to experience this extraordinary presentation.

John Wanamaker was a man who was willing to do things differently. His contribution was much more than a department store—through honesty, courtesy, fairness, and vision for a better world, he has left us all with a greater appreciation for excellence.

> *With humility and fear of the Lord*
> *come riches, honor, and life.*
> *Proverbs 22:4*

Mark Hamby